T0348142

©2021 The Shepherd Moon
Designed in Sydney, Australia

ISBN-13: 978-0-6485098-5-1

The collection includes the below selected works
in partnership with Red Room Poetry.

In the Small Hours
by Peter Boyle

A Kind of Paradise
by Mindy Gill

Know me in this moment
by Hadise Ansari

The Unspeakable
by Silverwater Poets

Cover Design
Lucas Cortet

The Shepherd Moon

theshepherdmoon.com

A POCKETFUL OF

# POEMS

# INTRODUCTION

Poetry, in a general sense, may be defined to be "the expression of the imagination": and poetry is connate with the origin of man. Man is an instrument over which a series of external and internal impressions are driven, like the alternations of an ever-changing wind over an Æolian lyre, which move it by their motion to ever-changing melody. But there is a principle within the human being, and perhaps within all sentient beings, which acts otherwise than in the lyre, and produces not melody alone, but harmony, by an internal adjustment of the sounds or motions thus excited to the impressions which excite them. It is as if the lyre could accommodate its chords to the motions of that which strikes them, in a determined proportion of sound; even as the musician can accommodate his voice to the sound of the lyre. A child at play by itself will express its delight by its voice and motions; and every inflexion of tone and every gesture will bear exact relation to a corresponding antitype in the pleasurable impressions which awakened it; it will be the reflected image of that impression; and as the lyre trembles and sounds after the wind has died away; so the child seeks, by prolonging in its voice and motions the duration of the effect, to prolong also a consciousness of the cause. In relation to the objects which delight a child these expressions are what poetry is to higher objects. The savage (for the savage is to ages what the child is to years) expresses the emotions produced in him by surrounding objects in a similar manner; and language and gesture, together with plastic or pictorial imitation, become the image of the combined effect of those objects, and of his apprehension of them. Man in society, with all his passions and his pleasures, next becomes the object of the passions and pleasures of man; an additional class of emotions produces an augmented treasure of expressions; and language, gesture, and the imitative arts, become at once the representation and the medium, the pencil and the picture, the chisel and the statute, the chord and the harmony. The social sympathies, or those laws from which, as from its elements, society results, begin to develop themselves from the moment that two human beings coexist; the future is contained within the present, as the plant within the seed; and equality, diversity, unity, contrast, mutual dependence, become the principles alone capable of affording the motives according to which the will of a social being is determined to action, inasmuch as he is social; and constitute pleasure in sensation, virtue in sentiment, beauty in art, truth in reasoning, and love in the intercourse of kind. Hence men, even in the infancy of society, observe a certain order in their words and actions, distinct from that of the objects and the impressions represented by them, all expression being subject to the laws of that from which it proceeds. But let us dismiss those more general considerations which might involve an inquiry into the principles of society itself, and restrict our view to the manner in which the imagination is expressed upon its forms.

In the youth of the world, men dance and sing and imitate natural objects observing in these actions, as in all others, a certain rhythm or order. And, although all men observe a similar, they observe not the same order, in the motions of the dance, in the melody of the song, in the combinations of language, in the series of their imitations of natural objects. For there is a certain order or rhythm belonging to each of these classes of mimetic representation, from which the hearer and the spectator receive an intenser and purer pleasure than from any other: the sense of an approximation to this order has been called taste by modern writers. Every man in the infancy of art observes an order which approximates more or less closely to that from which this highest delight results: but the diversity is not sufficiently marked, as that its gradations should be sensible, except in those instances where the predominance of this faculty of approximation to the beautiful (for so we may be permitted to name the relation between this highest pleasure and its cause) is very great. Those in whom it exists in excess are poets, in the most universal sense of the word; and the pleasure resulting from the manner in which they express the influence of society or nature upon their own minds, communicates itself to others, and gathers a sort of reduplication from that community. Their language is vitally metaphorical; that is, it marks the before unapprehended relations of things and perpetuates their apprehension, until the words which represent them, become, through time, signs for portions or classes of thoughts instead of pictures of integral thoughts; and then if no new poets should arise to create afresh the associations which have been thus disorganized, language will be dead to all the nobler purposes of human intercourse. These similitudes or relations are finely said by Lord Bacon to be "the same footsteps of nature impressed upon the various subjects of the world"—and he considers the faculty which perceives them as the store-house of axioms common to all knowledge. In the infancy of society every author is necessarily a poet, because language itself is poetry; and to be a poet is to apprehend the true and the beautiful, in a word, the good which exists in the relation, subsisting, first between existence and perception, and secondly between perception and expression. Every original language near to its source is in itself the chaos of a cyclic poem: the copiousness of lexicography and the distinctions of grammar are the works of a later age, and are merely the catalogue and the form of the creations of poetry.

But poets, or those who imagine and express this indestructible order, are not only the authors of language and of music, of the dance, and architecture, and statuary, and painting: they are the institutors of laws, and the founders of civil society, and the inventors of the arts of life, and the teachers, who draw into a certain propinquity with the beautiful and the true that partial apprehension of the agencies of the invisible world which is called religion. Hence all original religions are allegorical, or susceptible of allegory, and, like Janus, have a double face of false and true. Poets, according to the circumstances of the age and nation in which they appeared, were called, in the earlier epochs of the world, legislators, or prophets: a poet essentially comprises and unites both these characters. For he not only beholds intensely the present as it is, and discovers those laws according to which present things ought to be ordered, but he beholds the future in the present, and his thoughts are the germs of the flower and the fruit of latest time. Not that I assert poets to be prophets in the gross sense of the word, or that they can foretell the form as surely as they foreknow the spirit of events: such is the pretence of superstition, which would make poetry an attribute of prophecy, rather than prophecy an attribute of poetry. A poet participates in the eternal, the infinite, and the one; as far as relates to his conceptions, time and place and number are not. The grammatical forms which express the moods of time, and the difference of persons, and the distinction of place, are convertible with respect to the highest poetry without injuring it as poetry; and the choruses of Aeschylus, and the book of Job, and Dante's

"Paradise" would afford, more than any other writings, examples of this fact, if the limits of this essay did not forbid citation. The creations of sculpture, painting, and music are illustrations still more decisive.

Language, color, form, and religious and civil habits of action, are all the instruments and materials of poetry; they may be called poetry by that figure of speech which considers the effect as a synonym of the cause. But poetry in a more restricted sense expresses those arrangements of language, and especially metrical language, which are created by that imperial faculty, whose throne is curtained within the invisible nature of man. And this springs from the nature itself of language, which is a more direct representation of the actions and passions of our internal being, and is susceptible of more various and delicate combinations, than color, form, or motion, and is more plastic and obedient to the control of that faculty of which it is the creation. For language is arbitrarily produced by the imagination, and has relation to thoughts alone; but all other materials, instruments, and conditions of art have relations among each other, which limit and interpose between conception and expression. The former is as a mirror which reflects, the latter as a cloud which enfeebles, the light of which both are mediums of communication. Hence the fame of sculptors, painters, and musicians, although the intrinsic powers of the great masters of these arts may yield in no degree to that of those who have employed language as the hieroglyphic of their thoughts, has never equalled that of poets in the restricted sense of the term; as two performers of equal skill will produce unequal effects from a guitar and a harp. The fame of legislators and founders of religions, so long as their institutions last, alone seems to exceed that of poets in the restricted sense; but it can scarcely be a question, whether, if we deduct the celebrity which their flattery of the gross opinions of the vulgar usually conciliates, together with that which belonged to them in their higher character of poets, any excess will remain.

We have thus circumscribed the word poetry within the limits of that art which is the most familiar and the most perfect expression of the faculty itself. It is necessary, however, to make the circle still narrower, and to determine the distinction between measured and unmeasured language; for the popular division into prose and verse is inadmissible in accurate philosophy.

Sounds as well as thoughts have relation both between each other and towards that which they represent, and a perception of the order of those relations has always been found connected with a perception of the order of the relations of thoughts. Hence the language of poets has ever affected a certain uniform and harmonious recurrence of sound, without which it were not poetry, and which is scarcely less indispensable to the communication of its influence, than the words themselves, without reference to that peculiar order.

Hence the vanity of translation; it were as wise to cast a violet into a crucible that you might discover the formal principle of its color and odor, as seek to transfuse from one language into another the creations of a poet. The plant must spring again from its seed, or it will bear no flower—and this is the burden of the curse of Babel.

An observation of the regular mode of the recurrence of harmony in the language of poetical minds, together with its relation to music, produced metre, or a certain system of traditional forms of harmony and language. Yet it is by no means essential that a poet should accommodate his language to this traditional form, so that the harmony, which is its spirit, be observed. The practice is indeed convenient and popular, and to be preferred, especially in such composition as includes much action: but every great poet must inevitably innovate upon the example of his predecessors in the exact structure of his peculiar versification. The distinction between poets and prose writers is a vulgar error. The distinction between philosophers and poets has been anticipated. Plato was essentially a poet—the truth and splendor of his imagery, and the melody of his language, are the most intense that it is possible to conceive. He rejected the measure of the epic, dramatic, and lyrical forms, because he sought to kindle a harmony in thoughts divested of shape and action, and he forebore to invent any regular plan of rhythm which would include, under determinate forms, the varied pauses of his style. Cicero sought to imitate the cadence of his periods, but with little success. Lord Bacon was a poet. His language has a sweet and majestic rhythm, which satisfies the sense, no less than the almost superhuman wisdom of his philosophy satisfies the intellect; it is a strain which distends, and then bursts the circumference of the reader's mind, and pours itself forth together with it into the universal element with which it has perpetual sympathy. All the authors of revolutions in opinion are not only necessarily poets as they are inventors, nor even as their words unveil the permanent analogy of things by images which participate in the life of truth; but as their periods are harmonious and rhythmical, and contain in themselves the elements of verse; being the echo of the eternal music. Nor are those supreme poets, who have employed traditional forms of rhythm on account of the form and action of their subjects, less capable of perceiving and teaching the truth of things, than those who have omitted that form. Shakespeare, Dante, and Milton (to confine ourselves to modern writers) are philosophers of the very loftiest power.

A poem is the very image of life expressed in its eternal truth. There is this difference between a story and a poem, that a story is a catalogue of detached facts, which have no other connection than time, place, circumstance, cause and effect; the other is the creation of actions according to the unchangeable forms of human nature, as existing in the mind of the Creator, which is itself the image of all other minds. The one is partial, and applies only to a definite period of time, and a certain combination of events which can never again recur; the other is universal, and contains within itself the germ of a relation to whatever motives or actions have place in the possible varieties of human nature. Time, which destroys the beauty and the use of the story of particular facts, stripped of the poetry which should invest them, augments that of poetry, and forever develops new and wonderful applications of the eternal truth which it contains. Hence epitomes have been called the moths of just history; they eat out the poetry of it. A story of particular facts is as a mirror which obscures and distorts that which should be beautiful; poetry is a mirror which makes beautiful that which is distorted.

Percy Bysshe Shelley,
London, 1821

# Part I.

# The Experience of Life

## The Everlasting Voices

O sweet everlasting Voices, be still;
Go to the guards of the heavenly fold
And bid them wander obeying your will,
Flame under flame, till Time be no more;
Have you not heard that our hearts are old,
That you call in birds, in wind on the hill,
In shaken boughs, in tide on the shore?
O sweet everlasting Voices, be still.

WILLIAM BUTLER YEATS

# Life

The World's a bubble, and the Life of Man
    Less than a span:
In his conception wretched, from the womb
    So to the tomb;
Curst from his cradle, and brought up to years
    With cares and fears.
Who then to frail mortality shall trust,
But limns on water, or but writes in dust.

Yet whilst with sorrow here we live opprest,
    What life is best?
Courts are but only superficial schools
    To dandle fools:
The rural parts are turn'd into a den
    Of savage men:
And where's a city from foul vice so free,
But may be term'd the worst of all the three?

Domestic cares afflict the husband's bed,
    Or pains his head:
Those that live single, take it for a curse,
    Or do things worse:
Some would have children: those that have them, moan
    Or wish them gone:
What is it, then, to have, or have no wife,
But single thraldom, or a double strife?

Our own affections still at home to please
    Is a disease:
To cross the seas to any foreign soil,
    Peril and toil:
Wars with their noise affright us; when they cease,
    We are worse in peace;—
What then remains, but that we still should cry
For being born, or, being born, to die

LORD BACON

## Sudden Light

I have been here before,
But when or how I cannot tell:
I know the grass beyond the door,
The sweet keen smell,
The sighing sound, the lights around the shore.

You have been mine before,—
How long ago I may not know:
But just when at that swallow's soar
Your neck turn'd so,
Some veil did fall,—I knew it all of yore.

Has this been thus before?
And shall not thus time's eddying flight
Still with our lives our love restore
In death's despite,
And day and night yield one delight once more?

DANTE GABRIEL ROSSETTI

## The Children's Hour

Between the dark and the daylight,
    When the night is beginning to lower,
Comes a pause in the day's occupations,
    That is known as the Children's Hour.

I hear in the chamber above me
    The patter of little feet,
The sound of a door that is opened,
    And voices soft and sweet.

From my study I see in the lamplight,
    Descending the broad hall stair,
Grave Alice, and laughing Allegra,
    And Edith with golden hair.

A whisper, and then a silence:
    Yet I know by their merry eyes
They are plotting and planning together
    To take me by surprise.

A sudden rush from the stairway,
    A sudden raid from the hall!
By three doors left unguarded
    They enter my castle wall!

They climb up into my turret
    O'er the arms and back of my chair;
If I try to escape, they surround me;
    They seem to be everywhere.

They almost devour me with kisses,
    Their arms about me entwine,
Till I think of the Bishop of Bingen
    In his Mouse-Tower on the Rhine!

Do you think, O blue-eyed banditti,
    Because you have scaled the wall,
Such an old mustache as I am
    Is not a match for you all!

I have you fast in my fortress,
    And will not let you depart,
But put you down into the dungeon
    In the round-tower of my heart.

And there will I keep you forever,
    Yes, forever and a day,
Till the walls shall crumble to ruin,
    And moulder in dust away!

HENRY WADSWORTH LONGFELLOW

## Innocence

But that which most I wonder at, which most
I did esteem my bliss, which most I boast,
And ever shall enjoy, is that within
I felt no stain, nor spot of sin.

No darkness then did overshade,
    But all within was pure and bright,
No guilt did crush, nor fear invade
    But all my soul was full of light.

A joyful sense and purity
    Is all I can remember;
  The very night to me was bright,
    'Twas summer in December.

A serious meditation did employ
My soul within, which taken up with joy
Did seem no outward thing to note, but fly
All objects that do feed the eye.

While it those very objects did
    Admire, and prize, and praise, and love,
Which in their glory most are hid,
    Which presence only doth remove.

Their constant daily presence I
Rejoicing at, did see;
    And that which takes them from the eye
Of others, offer'd them to me.

No inward inclination did I feel
To avarice or pride: my soul did kneel
In admiration all the day. No lust, nor strife,
Polluted then my infant life.

No fraud nor anger in me mov'd,
    No malice, jealousy, or spite;
All that I saw I truly lov'd.
    Contentment only and delight

    Were in my soul. O Heav'n! what bliss
Did I enjoy and feel!
    What powerful delight did this
Inspire! for this I daily kneel.

Whether it be that nature is so pure,
And custom only vicious; or that sure
God did by miracle the guilt remove,
And make my soul to feel his love

So early: or that 'twas one day,
    Wherein this happiness I found;
Whose strength and brightness so do ray,
    That still it seems me to surround;

What ere it is, it is a light
    So endless unto me
That I a world of true delight
    Did then and to this day do see.

That prospect was the gate of Heav'n, that day
The ancient light of Eden did convey
Into my soul: I was an Adam there
A little Adam in a sphere

Of joys! O there my ravish'd sense
    Was entertain'd in Paradise,
And had a sight of innocence
    Which was beyond all bound and price.

An antepast of Heaven sure!
    I on the earth did reign;
Within, without me, all was pure;
    I must become a child again.

THOMAS TRAHERNE

## On Education

When infant Reason first exerts her sway,
And new-formed thoughts their earliest charms display;
Then let the growing race employ your care
Then guard their opening minds from Folly's snare;
Correct the rising passions of their youth,
Teach them each serious, each important truth;
Plant heavenly virtue in the tender breast,
Destroy each vice that might its growth molest;
Point out betimes the course they should pursue;
Then with redoubled pleasure shall you view
Their reason strengthen as their years increase,
Their virtue ripen and their follies cease;
Like corn sown early in the fertile soil,
The richest harvest shall repay your toil.

ELIZABETH BENTLEY

# Youth and Calm

Tis death! and peace, indeed, is here,
And ease from shame, and rest from fear.
There's nothing can dismarble now
The smoothness of that limpid brow.
But is a calm like this, in truth,
The crowning end of life and youth,
And when this boon rewards the dead,
Are all debts paid, has all been said?
And is the heart of youth so light,
Its step so firm, its eye so bright,
Because on its hot brow there blows
A wind of promise and repose
From the far grave, to which it goes;
Because it hath the hope to come,
One day, to harbour in the tomb?
Ah no, the bliss youth dreams is one
For daylight, for the cheerful sun,
For feeling nerves and living breath—
Youth dreams a bliss on this side death.
It dreams a rest, if not more deep,
More grateful than this marble sleep;
It hears a voice within it tell:
Calm's not life's crown, though calm is well.
Tis all perhaps which man acquires,
But 'tis not what our youth desires.

MATTHEW ARNOLD

## Live Blindly and upon the Hour

Live blindly and upon the hour. The Lord,
Who was the Future, died full long ago.
Knowledge which is the Past is folly. Go,
Poor child, and be not to thyself abhorred.
Around thine earth sun-wingèd winds do blow
And planets roll; a meteor draws his sword;
The rainbow breaks his seven-coloured chord
And the long strips of river-silver flow:
Awake! Give thyself to the lovely hours.
Drinking their lips, catch thou the dream in flight
About their fragile hairs' aërial gold.
Thou art divine, thou livest,—as of old
Apollo springing naked to the light,
And all his island shivered into flowers.

TRUMBULL STICKNEY

# Change

And this is what is left of youth! . . .
There were two boys, who were bred up together,
Shared the same bed, and fed at the same board;
Each tried the other's sport, from their first chase,
Young hunters of the butterfly and bee,
To when they followed the fleet hare, and tried
The swiftness of the bird. They lay beside
The silver trout stream, watching as the sun
Played on the bubbles: shared each in the store
Of either's garden: and together read
Of him, the master of the desert isle,
Till a low hut, a gun, and a canoe,
Bounded their wishes. Or if ever came
A thought of future days, 'twas but to say
That they would share each other's lot, and do
Wonders, no doubt. But this was vain: they parted
With promises of long remembrance, words
Whose kindness was the heart's, and those warm tears,
Hidden like shame by the young eyes which shed them,
But which are thought upon in after-years
As what we would give worlds to shed once more.

They met again, — but different from themselves,
At least what each remembered of themselves:
The one proud as a soldier of his rank,
And of his many battles: and the other
Proud of his Indian wealth, and of the skill
And toil which gathered it; each with a brow

And heart alike darkened by years and care.
They met with cold words, and yet colder looks:
Each was changed in himself, and yet each thought
The other only changed, himself the same.
And coldness bred dislike, and rivalry
Came like the pestilence o'er some sweet thoughts
That lingered yet, healthy and beautiful,
Amid dark and unkindly ones. And they,
Whose boyhood had not known one jarring word,
Were strangers in their age: if their eyes met,
'Twas but to look contempt, and when they spoke,
Their speech was wormwood! . . .
. . . And this, this is life!

LETITIA ELIZABETH LANDON

# The Salutation

These little limbs,
   These eyes and hands which here I find,
These rosy cheeks wherewith my life begins,
   Where have ye been? behind
What curtain were ye from me hid so long?
Where was, in what abyss, my speaking tongue?

   When silent I
   So many thousand, thousand years
Beneath the dust did in a chaos lie,
   How could I smiles or tears,
Or lips or hands or eyes or ears perceive?
Welcome ye treasures which I now receive.

   I that so long
   Was nothing from eternity,
Did little think such joys as ear or tongue
   To celebrate or see:
Such sounds to hear, such hands to feel, such feet,
Beneath the skies on such a ground to meet.

   New burnished joys,
   Which yellow gold and pearls excel!
Such sacred treasures are the limbs in boys,
   In which a soul doth dwell;
Their organizèd joints and azure veins
More wealth include than all the world contains.

From dust I rise,
   And out of nothing now awake;
These brighter regions which salute mine eyes,
   A gift from God I take.
The earth, the seas, the light, the day, the skies,
The sun and stars are mine if those I prize.

      Long time before
   I in my mother's womb was born,
A God, preparing, did this glorious store,
   The world, for me adorn.
Into this Eden so divine and fair,
So wide and bright, I come His son and heir.

      A stranger here
   Strange things doth meet, strange glories see;
Strange treasures lodged in this fair world appear,
   Strange all and new to me;
But that they mine should be, who nothing was,
That strangest is of all, yet brought to pass.

THOMAS TRAHERNE

## To a Child

The leaves talked in the twilight, dear;
  Hearken the tale they told:
How in some far-off place and year,
  Before the world grew old,

I was a dreaming forest tree,
  You were a wild, sweet bird
Who sheltered at the heart of me
  Because the north wind stirred;

How, when the chiding gale was still,
  When peace fell soft on fear,
You stayed one golden hour to fill
  My dream with singing, dear.

To-night the self-same songs are sung
  The first green forest heard;
My heart and the gray world grow young—
  To shelter you, my bird.

SOPHIE JEWETT

## The River of Life

The more we live, more brief appear
  Our life's succeeding stages:
A day to childhood seems a year,
  And years like passing ages.

The gladsome current of our youth
  Ere passion yet disorders,
Steals lingering like a river smooth
  Along its grassy borders.

But as the careworn cheek grows wan,
  And sorrow's shafts fly thicker,
Ye Stars, that measure life to man,
  Why seem your courses quicker?

When joys have lost their bloom and breath
  And life itself is vapid,
Why, as we reach the Falls of Death,
  Feel we its tide more rapid?

It may be strange—yet who would change
  Time's course to lower speeding,
When one by one our friends have gone
  And left our bosoms bleeding?

Heaven gives our years of fading strength
  Indemnifying fleetness;
And those of youth, a seeming length,
  Proportion'd to their sweetness.

THOMAS CAMPBELL

# In the Small Hours

It's three a.m. in the morning
of a day you won't enter for so many hours.
Where you are
yesterday's sunlight still bathes your feet as you walk
and tonight hearing your voice
I worried that one day
I'll lose my images of all those I love.
Outside the city's still restless:
taxis alert and shiny as golden birds
waiting for the crumbs of dawn.
At fifty five I know so little how to live.
In cafes across this city
lovers still hold hands
and cups balance on the edges of tables.
Darkness falls around me like soft snow.
Beside the narrow bed
my night-light is staring right into me.
I will hold your voice inside me as long as I can.
When I sleep you'll go on walking
through a steady explosion of white flowers.

PETER BOYLE

# Preludes

## I

The winter evening settles down
With smell of steaks in passageways.
Six o'clock.
The burnt-out ends of smoky days.
And now a gusty shower wraps
The grimy scraps
Of withered leaves about your feet
And newspapers from vacant lots;
The showers beat
On broken blinds and chimney-pots,
And at the corner of the street
A lonely cab-horse steams and stamps.

And then the lighting of the lamps.

## II

The morning comes to consciousness
Of faint stale smells of beer
From the sawdust-trampled street
With all its muddy feet that press
To early coffee-stands.
With the other masquerades

That time resumes,
One thinks of all the hands
That are raising dingy shades
In a thousand furnished rooms.

### III

You tossed a blanket from the bed,
You lay upon your back, and waited;
You dozed, and watched the night revealing
The thousand sordid images
Of which your soul was constituted;
They flickered against the ceiling.
And when all the world came back
And the light crept up between the shutters
And you heard the sparrows in the gutters,
You had such a vision of the street
As the street hardly understands;
Sitting along the bed's edge, where
You curled the papers from your hair,
Or clasped the yellow soles of feet
In the palms of both soiled hands.

### IV

His soul stretched tight across the skies
That fade behind a city block,
Or trampled by insistent feet
At four and five and six o'clock;

And short square fingers stuffing pipes,
And evening newspapers, and eyes
Assured of certain certainties,
The conscience of a blackened street
Impatient to assume the world.

I am moved by fancies that are curled
Around these images, and cling:
The notion of some infinitely gentle
Infinitely suffering thing.

Wipe your hand across your mouth, and laugh;
The worlds revolve like ancient women
Gathering fuel in vacant lots.

T. S. ELIOT

## The Human Seasons

Four Seasons fill the measure of the year;
   There are four seasons in the mind of man:
He has his lusty Spring, when fancy clear
   Takes in all beauty with an easy span:
He has his Summer, when luxuriously
   Spring's honied cud of youthful thought he loves
To ruminate, and by such dreaming high
   Is nearest unto heaven: quiet coves
His soul has in its Autumn, when his wings
   He furleth close; contented so to look
On mists in idleness—to let fair things
   Pass by unheeded as a threshold brook.
He has his Winter too of pale misfeature,
Or else he would forego his mortal nature.

JOHN KEATS

## The Old Familiar Faces

I have had playmates, I have had companions,
In my days of childhood, in my joyful school-days,
All, all are gone, the old familiar faces.

I have been laughing, I have been carousing,
Drinking late, sitting late, with my bosom cronies,
All, all are gone, the old familiar faces.

I loved a love once, fairest among women;
Closed are her doors on me, I must not see her —
All, all are gone, the old familiar faces.

I have a friend, a kinder friend has no man;
Like an ingrate, I left my friend abruptly;
Left him, to muse on the old familiar faces.

Ghost-like, I paced round the haunts of my childhood.
Earth seemed a desert I was bound to traverse,
Seeking to find the old familiar faces.

Friend of my bosom, thou more than a brother,
Why wert not thou born in my father's dwelling?
So might we talk of the old familiar faces —

How some they have died, and some they have left me,
And some are taken from me; all are departed;
All, all are gone, the old familiar faces.

CHARLES LAMB

# Experience

## I

Like Crusoe with the bootless gold we stand
Upon the desert verge of death, and say:
"What shall avail the woes of yesterday
To buy to-morrow's wisdom, in the land
Whose currency is strange unto our hand?
In life's small market they had served to pay
Some late-found rapture, could we but delay
Till Time hath matched our means to our demand."

But otherwise Fate wills it, for, behold,
Our gathered strength of individual pain,
When Time's long alchemy hath made it gold,
Dies with us—hoarded all these years in vain,
Since those that might be heir to it the mould
Renew, and coin themselves new griefs again.

## II

O Death, we come full-handed to thy gate,
Rich with strange burden of the mingled years,
Gains and renunciations, mirth and tears,
And love's oblivion, and remembering hate,
Nor know we what compulsion laid such freight
Upon our souls—and shall our hopes and fears
Buy nothing of thee, Death? Behold our wares,
And sell us the one joy for which we wait.

Had we lived longer, like had such for sale,
With the last coin of sorrow purchased cheap,
But now we stand before thy shadowy pale,
And all our longings lie within thy keep—
Death, can it be the years shall naught avail?

"Not so," Death answered, "they shall purchase sleep."

EDITH WHARTON

## The Heart of the Night

From child to youth; from youth to arduous man;
From lethargy to fever of the heart;
From faithful life to dream-dower'd days apart;
From trust to doubt; from doubt to brink of ban;—
Thus much of change in one swift cycle ran
Till now. Alas, the soul!—how soon must she
Accept her primal immortality,—
The flesh resume its dust whence it began?

O Lord of work and peace! O Lord of life!
O Lord, the awful Lord of will! though late,
Even yet renew this soul with duteous breath:
That when the peace is garner'd in from strife,
The work retriev'd, the will regenerate,
This soul may see thy face, O Lord of death!

DANTE GABRIEL ROSSETTI

## Before the Mirror

Now like the Lady of Shalott,
  I dwell within an empty room,
And through the day and through the night
  I sit before an ancient loom.

And like the Lady of Shalott
  I look into a mirror wide,
Where shadows come, and shadows go,
  And ply my shuttle as they glide.

Not as she wove the yellow wool,
  Ulysses' wife, Penelope;
By day a queen among her maids,
  But in the night a woman, she,

Who, creeping from her lonely couch,
  Unraveled all the slender woof;
Or, with a torch, she climbed the towers,
  To fire the fagots on the roof!

But weaving with a steady hand
  The shadows, whether false or true,
I put aside a doubt which asks
  'Among these phantoms what are you?'

For not with altar, tomb, or urn,
   Or long-haired Greek with hollow shield,
Or dark-prowed ship with banks of oars,
   Or banquet in the tented field;

Or Norman knight in armor clad,
   Waiting a foe where four roads meet;
Or hawk and hound in bosky dell,
   Where dame and page in secret greet;

Or rose and lily, bud and flower,
   My web is broidered. Nothing bright
Is woven here: the shadows grow
   Still darker in the mirror's light!

And as my web grows darker too,
   Accursed seems this empty room;
For still I must forever weave
   These phantoms by this ancient loom.

ELIZABETH DREW BARSTOW STODDARD

# Fate

That you are fair or wise is vain,
Or strong, or rich, or generous;
You must have also the untaught strain
That sheds beauty on the rose.
There is a melody born of melody,
Which melts the world into a sea:
Toil could never compass it;
Art its height could never hit;
It came never out of wit;
But a music music-born
Well may Jove and Juno scorn.
Thy beauty, if it lack the fire
Which drives me mad with sweet desire,
What boots it? what the soldier's mail,
Unless he conquer and prevail?
What all the goods thy pride which lift,
If thou pine for another's gift?
Alas! that one is born in blight,
Victim of perpetual slight:
When thou lookest on his face,
Thy heart saith, "Brother, go thy ways!
None shall ask thee what thou doest,
Or care a rush for what thou knowest,
Or listen when thou repliest,
Or remember where thou liest,
Or how thy supper is sodden;"
And another is born
To make the sun forgotten.

Surely he carries a talisman
Under his tongue;
Broad are his shoulders, and strong;
And his eye is scornful,
Threatening, and young.
I hold it of little matter
Whether your jewel be of pure water,
A rose diamond or a white,
But whether it dazzle me with light.
I care not how you are dressed,
In the coarsest or in the best;
Nor whether your name is base or brave;
Nor for the fashion of your behavior;
But whether you charm me,
Bid my bread feed and my fire warm me,
And dress up Nature in your favor.
One thing is forever good;
That one thing is Success, —
Dear to the Eumenides,
And to all the heavenly brood.
Who bides at home, nor looks abroad,
Carries the eagles, and masters the sword.

RALPH WALDO EMERSON

## Growing Old

What is it to grow old?
Is it to lose the glory of the form,
The luster of the eye?
Is it for beauty to forego her wreath?
—Yes, but not this alone.

Is it to feel our strength—
Not our bloom only, but our strength—decay?
Is it to feel each limb
Grow stiffer, every function less exact,
Each nerve more loosely strung?

Yes, this, and more; but not
Ah, 'tis not what in youth we dreamed 'twould be!
'Tis not to have our life
Mellowed and softened as with sunset glow,
A golden day's decline.

'Tis not to see the world
As from a height, with rapt prophetic eyes,
And heart profoundly stirred;
And weep, and feel the fullness of the past,
The years that are no more.

It is to spend long days
And not once feel that we were ever young;
It is to add, immured
In the hot prison of the present, month
To month with weary pain.

It is to suffer this,
And feel but half, and feebly, what we feel.
Deep in our hidden heart
Festers the dull remembrance of a change,
But no emotion—none.

It is—last stage of all—
When we are frozen up within, and quite
The phantom of ourselves,
To hear the world applaud the hollow ghost
Which blamed the living man.

MATTHEW ARNOLD

## The Light of Other Days

Oft, in the stilly night,
 Ere slumber's chain has bound me,
Fond Memory brings the light
 Of other days around me:
   The smiles, the tears
   Of boyhood's years,
 The words of love then spoken;
   The eyes that shone,
   Now dimm'd and gone,
 The cheerful hearts now broken!
Thus in the stilly night,
 Ere slumber's chain has bound me,
Sad Memory brings the light
 Of other days around me.
When I remember all
 The friends, so link'd together,
I've seen around me fall
 Like leaves in wintry weather,
   I feel like one
   Who treads alone
 Some banquet-hall deserted,
   Whose lights are fled,
   Whose garlands dead,
 And all but he departed!
Thus in the stilly night,
 Ere slumber's chain has bound me,
Sad Memory brings the light
 Of other days around me.

THOMAS MOORE

## Time Long Past

Like the ghost of a dear friend dead
Is Time long past.
A tone which is now forever fled,
A hope which is now forever past,
A love so sweet it could not last,
Was Time long past.

There were sweet dreams in the night
Of Time long past:
And, was it sadness or delight,
Each day a shadow onward cast
Which made us wish it yet might last—
That Time long past.

There is regret, almost remorse,
For Time long past.
Tis like a child's belovèd corse
A father watches, till at last
Beauty is like remembrance, cast
From Time long past.

PERCY BYSSHE SHELLEY

## The Day is Done

The day is done, and the darkness
   Falls from the wings of Night,
As a feather is wafted downward
   From an eagle in his flight.

I see the lights of the village
   Gleam through the rain and the mist,
And a feeling of sadness comes o'er me
   That my soul cannot resist:

A feeling of sadness and longing,
   That is not akin to pain,
And resembles sorrow only
   As the mist resembles the rain.

Come, read to me some poem,
   Some simple and heartfelt lay,
That shall soothe this restless feeling,
   And banish the thoughts of day.

Not from the grand old masters,
   Not from the bards sublime,
Whose distant footsteps echo
   Through the corridors of Time.

For, like strains of martial music,
    Their mighty thoughts suggest
Life's endless toil and endeavor;
    And to-night I long for rest.

Read from some humbler poet,
    Whose songs gushed from his heart,
As showers from the clouds of summer,
    Or tears from the eyelids start;

Who, through long days of labor,
    And nights devoid of ease,
Still heard in his soul the music
    Of wonderful melodies.

Such songs have power to quiet
    The restless pulse of care,
And come like the benediction
    That follows after prayer.

Then read from the treasured volume
    The poem of thy choice,
And lend to the rhyme of the poet
    The beauty of thy voice.

And the night shall be filled with music,
    And the cares, that infest the day,
Shall fold their tents, like the Arabs,
    And as silently steal away.

HENRY WADSWORTH LONGFELLOW

## The Buried Life

Light flows our war of mocking words, and yet,
Behold, with tears mine eyes are wet!
I feel a nameless sadness o'er me roll.
Yes, yes, we know that we can jest,
We know, we know that we can smile!
But there's a something in this breast,
To which thy light words bring no rest,
And thy gay smiles no anodyne.
Give me thy hand, and hush awhile,
And turn those limpid eyes on mine,
And let me read there, love! thy inmost soul.

Alas! is even love too weak
To unlock the heart, and let it speak?
Are even lovers powerless to reveal
To one another what indeed they feel?
I knew the mass of men conceal'd
Their thoughts, for fear that if reveal'd
They would by other men be met
With blank indifference, or with blame reproved;
I knew they lived and moved
Trick'd in disguises, alien to the rest
Of men, and alien to themselves—and yet
The same heart beats in every human breast!

But we, my love!—doth a like spell benumb
Our hearts, our voices?—must we too be dumb?

Ah! well for us, if even we,
Even for a moment, can get free
Our heart, and have our lips unchain'd;
For that which seals them hath been deep-ordain'd!

Fate, which foresaw
How frivolous a baby man would be—
By what distractions he would be possess'd,
How he would pour himself in every strife,
And well-nigh change his own identity—
That it might keep from his capricious play
His genuine self, and force him to obey
Even in his own despite his being's law,
Bade through the deep recesses of our breast
The unregarded river of our life
Pursue with indiscernible flow its way;
And that we should not see
The buried stream, and seem to be
Eddying at large in blind uncertainty,
Though driving on with it eternally.

But often, in the world's most crowded streets,
But often, in the din of strife,
There rises an unspeakable desire
After the knowledge of our buried life;
A thirst to spend our fire and restless force
In tracking out our true, original course;

A longing to inquire
Into the mystery of this heart which beats
So wild, so deep in us—to know
Whence our lives come and where they go.
And many a man in his own breast then delves,
But deep enough, alas! none ever mines.
And we have been on many thousand lines,
And we have shown, on each, spirit and power;
But hardly have we, for one little hour,
Been on our own line, have we been ourselves—
Hardly had skill to utter one of all
The nameless feelings that course through our breast,
But they course on for ever unexpress'd.
And long we try in vain to speak and act
Our hidden self, and what we say and do
Is eloquent, is well—but 't is not true!
And then we will no more be rack'd
With inward striving, and demand
Of all the thousand nothings of the hour
Their stupefying power;
Ah yes, and they benumb us at our call!
Yet still, from time to time, vague and forlorn,
From the soul's subterranean depth upborne
As from an infinitely distant land,
Come airs, and floating echoes, and convey
A melancholy into all our day.
Only—but this is rare—
When a belovèd hand is laid in ours,
When, jaded with the rush and glare
Of the interminable hours,

Our eyes can in another's eyes read clear,
When our world-deafen'd ear
Is by the tones of a loved voice caress'd—
A bolt is shot back somewhere in our breast,
And a lost pulse of feeling stirs again.
The eye sinks inward, and the heart lies plain,
And what we mean, we say, and what we would, we
    know.
A man becomes aware of his life's flow,
And hears its winding murmur; and he sees
The meadows where it glides, the sun, the breeze.

And there arrives a lull in the hot race
Wherein he doth for ever chase
That flying and elusive shadow, rest.
An air of coolness plays upon his face,
And an unwonted calm pervades his breast.
And then he thinks he knows
The hills where his life rose,
And the sea where it goes.

MATTHEW ARNOLD

## The Dead Man Walking

They hail me as one living,
But don't they know
That I have died of late years,
Untombed although?

I am but a shape that stands here,
A pulseless mould,
A pale past picture, screening
Ashes gone cold.

Not at a minute's warning,
Not in a loud hour,
For me ceased Time's enchantments
In hall and bower.

There was no tragic transit,
No catch of breath,
When silent seasons inched me
On to this death ....

— A Troubadour-youth I rambled
With Life for lyre,
The beats of being raging
In me like fire.

But when I practised eyeing
The goal of men,
It iced me, and I perished
A little then.

When passed my friend, my kinsfolk,
Through the Last Door,
And left me standing bleakly,
I died yet more;

And when my Love's heart kindled
In hate of me,
Wherefore I knew not, died I
One more degree.

And if when I died fully
I cannot say,
And changed into the corpse-thing
I am to-day,

Yet is it that, though whiling
The time somehow
In walking, talking, smiling,
I live not now.

THOMAS HARDY

# My Days among the Dead are Past

My days among the Dead are past;
   Around me I behold,
Where'er these casual eyes are cast,
   The mighty minds of old;
My never-failing friends are they,
With whom I converse day by day.

With them I take delight in weal,
   And seek relief in woe;
And while I understand and feel
   How much to them I owe,
My cheeks have often been bedew'd
With tears of thoughtful gratitude.

My thoughts are with the Dead, with them
   I live in long-past years,
Their virtues love, their faults condemn,
   Partake their hopes and fears,
And from their lessons seek and find
Instruction with an humble mind.

My hopes are with the Dead, anon
   My place with them will be,
And I with them shall travel on
   Through all Futurity;
Yet leaving here a name, I trust,
That will not perish in the dust.

ROBERT SOUTHEY

"Oh could I raise the darken'd veil"

Oh could I raise the darken'd veil,
Which hides my future life from me,
Could unborn ages slowly sail,
Before my view—and could I see
My every action painted there,
To cast one look I would not dare.
There poverty and grief might stand,
And dark Despair's corroding hand,
Would make me seek the lonely tomb
To slumber in its endless gloom.
Then let me never cast a look,
Within Fate's fix'd mysterious book.

NATHANIEL HAWTHORNE

## Faith

Better trust all, and be deceived,
  And weep that trust, and that deceiving;
Than doubt one heart, that, if believed,
  Had blessed one's life with true believing.

Oh, in this mocking world, too fast
  The doubting fiend o'ertakes our youth!
Better be cheated to the last,
  Than lose the blessèd hope of truth.

FRANCES ANNE KEMBLE

This World is not Conclusion

This World is not Conclusion.
A Species stands beyond -
Invisible, as Music -
But positive, as Sound -
It beckons, and it baffles -
Philosophy, dont know -
And through a Riddle, at the last -
Sagacity, must go -
To guess it, puzzles scholars -
To gain it, Men have borne
Contempt of Generations
And Crucifixion, shown -
Faith slips - and laughs, and rallies -
Blushes, if any see -
Plucks at a twig of Evidence -
And asks a Vane, the way -
Much Gesture, from the Pulpit -
Strong Hallelujahs roll -
Narcotics cannot still the Tooth
That nibbles at the soul -

EMILY DICKINSON

# Epilogue

At the midnight in the silence of the sleep-time,
When you set your fancies free,
Will they pass to where—by death, fools think,
    imprisoned—
Low he lies who once so loved you, whom you loved so,
—Pity me?

Oh to love so, be so loved, yet so mistaken!
What had I on earth to do
With the slothful, with the mawkish, the unmanly?
Like the aimless, helpless, hopeless, did I drivel
—Being—who?

One who never turned his back but marched breast
    forward,
Never doubted clouds would break,
Never dreamed, though right were worsted, wrong
    would triumph,
Held we fall to rise, are baffled to fight better,
Sleep to wake.

No, at noonday in the bustle of man's work-time
Greet the unseen with a cheer!
Bid him forward, breast and back as either should be,
Strive and thrive! cry "Speed,—fight on, fare ever
There as here!"

ROBERT BROWNING

# Part II

# Travel and Discovery

## Upon Westminster Bridge

*September 3, 1802*

Earth has not anything to show more fair:
Dull would he be of soul who could pass by
A sight so touching in its majesty:
This City now doth, like a garment, wear
The beauty of the morning; silent, bare,
Ships, towers, domes, theatres, and temples lie
Open unto the fields, and to the sky;
All bright and glittering in the smokeless air.
Never did sun more beautifully steep
In his first splendour, valley, rock, or hill;
Ne'er saw I, never felt, a calm so deep!
The river glideth at his own sweet will:
Dear God! the very houses seem asleep;
And all that mighty heart is lying still!

WILLIAM WORDSWORTH

## Ozymandias

I met a traveller from an antique land
Who said: "Two vast and trunkless legs of stone
Stand in the desert . . . Near them, on the sand,
Half sunk, a shattered visage lies, whose frown,
And wrinkled lip, and sneer of cold command,
Tell that its sculptor well those passions read
Which yet survive, stamped on these lifeless things,
The hand that mocked them, and the heart that fed:
And on the pedestal these words appear:
My name is Ozymandias, king of kings:
Look on my works, ye Mighty, and despair!'
Nothing beside remains. Round the decay
Of that colossal wreck, boundless and bare
The lone and level sands stretch far away."

PERCY BYSSHE SHELLEY

# I Wandered Lonely as a Cloud

I wandered lonely as a cloud
That floats on high o'er vales and hills,
When all at once I saw a crowd,
A host, of golden daffodils;
Beside the lake, beneath the trees,
Fluttering and dancing in the breeze.

Continuous as the stars that shine
And twinkle on the milky way,
They stretched in never-ending line
Along the margin of a bay:
Ten thousand saw I at a glance,
Tossing their heads in sprightly dance.

The waves beside them danced; but they
Out-did the sparkling waves in glee:
A poet could not but be gay,
In such a jocund company:
I gazed—and gazed—but little thought
What wealth the show to me had brought:

For oft, when on my couch I lie
In vacant or in pensive mood,
They flash upon that inward eye
Which is the bliss of solitude;
And then my heart with pleasure fills,
And dances with the daffodils.

WILLIAM WORDSWORTH

# The Brook

I come from haunts of coot and hern,
　I make a sudden sally
And sparkle out among the fern,
　To bicker down a valley.

By thirty hills I hurry down,
　Or slip between the ridges,
By twenty thorpes, a little town,
　And half a hundred bridges.

Till last by Philip's farm I flow
　To join the brimming river,
For men may come and men may go,
　But I go on for ever.

I chatter over stony ways,
　In little sharps and trebles,
I bubble into eddying bays,
　I babble on the pebbles.

With many a curve my banks I fret
　By many a field and fallow,
And many a fairy foreland set
　With willow-weed and mallow.

I chatter, chatter, as I flow
  To join the brimming river,
For men may come and men may go,
  But I go on for ever.

I wind about, and in and out,
  With here a blossom sailing,
And here and there a lusty trout,
  And here and there a grayling,

And here and there a foamy flake
  Upon me, as I travel
With many a silvery waterbreak
  Above the golden gravel,

And draw them all along, and flow
  To join the brimming river
For men may come and men may go,
  But I go on for ever.

I steal by lawns and grassy plots,
  I slide by hazel covers;
I move the sweet forget-me-nots
  That grow for happy lovers.

I slip, I slide, I gloom, I glance,
  Among my skimming swallows;
I make the netted sunbeam dance
  Against my sandy shallows.

I murmur under moon and stars
   In brambly wildernesses;
I linger by my shingly bars;
   I loiter round my cresses;

And out again I curve and flow
   To join the brimming river,
For men may come and men may go,
   But I go on for ever.

LORD TENNYSON

## The Sign-Post

The dim sea glints chill. The white sun is shy,
And the skeleton weeds and the never-dry,
Rough, long grasses keep white with frost
At the hilltop by the finger-post;
The smoke of the traveller's-joy is puffed
Over hawthorn berry and hazel tuft.
I read the sign. Which way shall I go?
A voice says: You would not have doubted so
At twenty. Another voice gentle with scorn
Says: At twenty you wished you had never been born.

One hazel lost a leaf of gold
From a tuft at the tip, when the first voice told
The other he wished to know what 'twould be
To be sixty by this same post. "You shall see,"
He laughed—and I had to join his laughter—
"You shall see; but either before or after,
Whatever happens, it must befall,
A mouthful of earth to remedy all
Regrets and wishes shall freely be given;
And if there be a flaw in that heaven
'Twill be freedom to wish, and your wish may be
To be here or anywhere talking to me,
No matter what the weather, on earth,
At any age between death and birth,
To see what day or night can be,
The sun and the frost, the land and the sea,
Summer, Autumn, Winter, Spring,—

With a poor man of any sort, down to a king,
Standing upright out in the air
Wondering where he shall journey, O where?"

EDWARD THOMAS

# The Road Not Taken

Two roads diverged in a yellow wood,
And sorry I could not travel both
And be one traveler, long I stood
And looked down one as far as I could
To where it bent in the undergrowth;

Then took the other, as just as fair,
And having perhaps the better claim,
Because it was grassy and wanted wear;
Though as for that the passing there
Had worn them really about the same,

And both that morning equally lay
In leaves no step had trodden black.
Oh, I kept the first for another day!
Yet knowing how way leads on to way,
I doubted if I should ever come back.

I shall be telling this with a sigh
Somewhere ages and ages hence:
Two roads diverged in a wood, and I—
I took the one less traveled by,
And that has made all the difference.

ROBERT FROST

## Up-Hill

Does the road wind up-hill all the way?
  Yes, to the very end.
Will the day's journey take the whole long day?
  From morn to night, my friend.

But is there for the night a resting-place?
  A roof for when the slow dark hours begin.
May not the darkness hide it from my face?
  You cannot miss that inn.

Shall I meet other wayfarers at night?
  Those who have gone before.
Then must I knock, or call when just in sight?
  They will not keep you standing at that door.

Shall I find comfort, travel-sore and weak?
  Of labour you shall find the sum.
Will there be beds for me and all who seek?
  Yea, beds for all who come.

CHRISTINA ROSSETTI

# Walking

To walk abroad is, not with eyes,
But thoughts, the fields to see and prize;
Else may the silent feet,
Like logs of wood,
Move up and down, and see no good
Nor joy nor glory meet.

Ev'n carts and wheels their place do change,
But cannot see, though very strange
The glory that is by;
Dead puppets may
Move in the bright and glorious day,
Yet not behold the sky.

And are not men than they more blind,
Who having eyes yet never find
The bliss in which they move;
Like statues dead
They up and down are carried
Yet never see nor love.

To walk is by a thought to go;
To move in spirit to and fro;
To mind the good we see;
To taste the sweet;
Observing all the things we meet
How choice and rich they be.

To note the beauty of the day,
And golden fields of corn survey;
Admire each pretty flow'r
With its sweet smell;
To praise their Maker, and to tell
The marks of his great pow'r.

To fly abroad like active bees,
Among the hedges and the trees,
To cull the dew that lies
On ev'ry blade,
From ev'ry blossom; till we lade
Our minds, as they their thighs.

Observe those rich and glorious things,
The rivers, meadows, woods, and springs,
The fructifying sun;
To note from far
The rising of each twinkling star
For us his race to run.

A little child these well perceives,
Who, tumbling in green grass and leaves,
May rich as kings be thought,
But there's a sight
Which perfect manhood may delight,
To which we shall be brought.

While in those pleasant paths we talk,
'Tis that tow'rds which at last we walk;

For we may by degrees
Wisely proceed
Pleasures of love and praise to heed,
From viewing herbs and trees.

THOMAS TRAHERNE

## Across the Border

*I have read somewhere that the birds of*
*fairyland are white as snow.* —*W. B. Yeats*

Where all the trees bear golden flowers,
　And all the birds are white;
Where fairy folk in dancing hours
　Burn stars for candlelight;

Where every wind and leaf can talk,
　But no man understand
Save one whose child-feet chanced to walk
　Green paths of fairyland;

I followed two swift silver wings;
　I stalked a roving song;
I startled shining, silent things;
　I wandered all day long.

But when it seemed the shadowy hours
　Whispered of soft-foot night,
I crept home to sweet common flowers,
　Brown birds, and candlelight.

SOPHIE JEWETT

# I Travelled among Unknown Men

I travelled among unknown men,
In lands beyond the sea;
Nor, England! did I know till then
What love I bore to thee.

Tis past, that melancholy dream!
Nor will I quit thy shore
A second time; for still I seem
To love thee more and more.

Among thy mountains did I feel
The joy of my desire;
And she I cherished turned her wheel
Beside an English fire.

Thy mornings showed, thy nights concealed,
The bowers where Lucy played;
And thine too is the last green field
That Lucy's eyes surveyed.

WILLIAM WORDSWORTH

## Home-Thoughts, from Abroad

Oh, to be in England
Now that April's there,
And whoever wakes in England
Sees, some morning, unaware,
That the lowest boughs and the brushwood sheaf
Round the elm-tree bole are in tiny leaf,
While the chaffinch sings on the orchard bough
In England—now!

And after April, when May follows,
And the whitethroat builds, and all the swallows!
Hark, where my blossomed pear-tree in the hedge
Leans to the field and scatters on the clover
Blossoms and dewdrops—at the bent spray's edge—
That's the wise thrush; he sings each song twice over,
Lest you should think he never could recapture
The first fine careless rapture!
And though the fields look rough with hoary dew,
All will be gay when noontide wakes anew
The buttercups, the little children's dower
—Far brighter than this gaudy melon-flower!

ROBERT BROWNING

## Admonition to a Traveller

Yes, there is holy pleasure in thine eye!
—The lovely cottage in the guardian nook
Hath stirr'd thee deeply; with its own dear brook,
Its own small pasture, almost its own sky!

But covet not the abode—O do not sigh
As many do, repining while they look;
Intruders who would tear from Nature's book
This precious leaf with harsh impiety:

—Think what the home would be if it were thine,
Even thine, though few thy wants!—Roof,
    window, door,
The very flowers are sacred to the Poor,

The roses to the porch which they entwine:
Yea, all that now enchants thee, from the day
On which it should be touch'd would melt away!

WILLIAM WORDSWORTH

# Eldorado

Gaily bedight,
  A gallant knight,
In sunshine and in shadow,
  Had journeyed long,
  Singing a song,
In search of Eldorado.

But he grew old—
  This knight so bold—
And o'er his heart a shadow—
  Fell as he found
  No spot of ground
That looked like Eldorado.

And, as his strength
  Failed him at length,
He met a pilgrim shadow—
  'Shadow,' said he,
  'Where can it be—
This land of Eldorado?'

'Over the Mountains
  Of the Moon,
Down the Valley of the Shadow,
  Ride, boldly ride,'
  The shade replied,—
'If you seek for Eldorado!'

EDGAR ALLAN POE

## By the Sea

It is a beauteous evening, calm and free;
The holy time is quiet as a nun
Breathless with adoration; the broad sun
Is sinking down in its tranquillity;

The gentleness of heaven is on the Sea:
Listen! the mighty being is awake,
And doth with his eternal motion make
A sound like thunder—everlastingly.

Dear child! dear girl! that walkest with me here,
If thou appear untouch'd by solemn thought
Thy nature is not therefore less divine:

Thou liest in Abraham's bosom all the year;
And worshipp'st at the Temple's inner shrine,
God being with thee when we know it not.

WILLIAM WORDSWORTH

# The Mermaid Tavern

Souls of Poets dead and gone
What Elysium have ye known,
Happy field or mossy cavern,
Choicer than the Mermaid Tavern?
Have ye tippled drink more fine
Than mine host's Canary wine?
Or are fruits of Paradise
Sweeter than those dainty pies
Of Venison? O generous food!
Drest as though bold Robin Hood
Would, with his Maid Marian,
Sup and browse from horn and can.

I have heard that on a day
Mine host's signboard flew away
Nobody knew whither, till
An astrologer's old quill
To a sheepskin gave the story—
Said he saw you in your glory
Underneath a new-old Sign
Sipping beverage divine,
And pledging with contented smack
The Mermaid in the Zodiac!

Souls of poets dead and gone
What Elysium have ye known—
Happy field or mossy cavern—
Choicer than the Mermaid Tavern?

JOHN KEATS

## Cape Cod

The low sandy beach and the thin scrub pine,
The wide reach of bay and the long sky line,—
O, I am sick for home!

The salt, salt smell of the thick sea air,
And the smooth round stones that the ebbtides wear,—
When will the good ship come?

The wretched stumps all charred and burned,
And the deep soft rut where the cartwheel turned,—
Why is the world so old?

The lapping wave, and the broad gray sky
Where the cawing crows and the slow gulls fly,
Where are the dead untold?

The thin, slant willows by the flooded bog,
The huge stranded hulk and the floating log,
Sorrow with life began!

And among the dark pines, and along the flat shore,
O the wind, and the wind, for evermore!
What will become of man?

GEORGE SANTAYANA

# Ulysses

It little profits that an idle king,
By this still hearth, among these barren crags,
Match'd with an aged wife, I mete and dole
Unequal laws unto a savage race,
That hoard, and sleep, and feed, and know not me.
I cannot rest from travel: I will drink
Life to the lees: All times I have enjoy'd
Greatly, have suffer'd greatly, both with those
That loved me, and alone, on shore, and when
Thro' scudding drifts the rainy Hyades
Vext the dim sea: I am become a name;
For always roaming with a hungry heart
Much have I seen and known; cities of men
And manners, climates, councils, governments,
Myself not least, but honour'd of them all;
And drunk delight of battle with my peers,
Far on the ringing plains of windy Troy.
I am a part of all that I have met;
Yet all experience is an arch wherethro'
Gleams that untravell'd world whose margin fades
For ever and forever when I move.
How dull it is to pause, to make an end,
To rust unburnish'd, not to shine in use!
As tho' to breathe were life! Life piled on life
Were all too little, and of one to me
Little remains: but every hour is saved
From that eternal silence, something more,
A bringer of new things; and vile it were

For some three suns to store and hoard myself,
And this gray spirit yearning in desire
To follow knowledge like a sinking star,
Beyond the utmost bound of human thought.

This is my son, mine own Telemachus,
To whom I leave the sceptre and the isle,—
Well-loved of me, discerning to fulfil
This labour, by slow prudence to make mild
A rugged people, and thro' soft degrees
Subdue them to the useful and the good.
Most blameless is he, centred in the sphere
Of common duties, decent not to fail
In offices of tenderness, and pay
Meet adoration to my household gods,
When I am gone. He works his work, I mine.

There lies the port; the vessel puffs her sail:
There gloom the dark, broad seas. My mariners,
Souls that have toil'd, and wrought, and thought with
    me—
That ever with a frolic welcome took
The thunder and the sunshine, and opposed
Free hearts, free foreheads—you and I are old;
Old age hath yet his honour and his toil;
Death closes all: but something ere the end,
Some work of noble note, may yet be done,
Not unbecoming men that strove with Gods.
The lights begin to twinkle from the rocks:
The long day wanes: the slow moon climbs: the deep

Moans round with many voices. Come, my friends,
T is not too late to seek a newer world.
Push off, and sitting well in order smite
The sounding furrows; for my purpose holds
To sail beyond the sunset, and the baths
Of all the western stars, until I die.
It may be that the gulfs will wash us down:
It may be we shall touch the Happy Isles,
And see the great Achilles, whom we knew.
Tho' much is taken, much abides; and tho'
We are not now that strength which in old days
Moved earth and heaven, that which we are, we are;
One equal temper of heroic hearts,
Made weak by time and fate, but strong in will
To strive, to seek, to find, and not to yield.

LORD TENNYSON

# A Boat Beneath a Sunny Sky

A boat beneath a sunny sky,
Lingering onward dreamily
In an evening of July —

Children three that nestle near,
Eager eye and willing ear,
Pleased a simple tale to hear —

Long has paled that sunny sky:
Echoes fade and memories die:
Autumn frosts have slain July.

Still she haunts me, phantomwise,
Alice moving under skies
Never seen by waking eyes.

Children yet, the tale to hear,
Eager eye and willing ear,
Lovingly shall nestle near.

In a Wonderland they lie,
Dreaming as the days go by,
Dreaming as the summers die:

Ever drifting down the stream —
Lingering in the golden gleam —
Life, what is it but a dream?

LEWIS CARROLL

# The Chambered Nautilus

This is the ship of pearl, which, poets feign,
Sails the unshadowed main,—
The venturous bark that flings
On the sweet summer wind its purpled wings
In gulfs enchanted, where the Siren sings,
And coral reefs lie bare,
Where the cold sea-maids rise to sun their streaming
    hair.

Its webs of living gauze no more unfurl;
Wrecked is the ship of pearl!
And every chambered cell,
Where its dim dreaming life was wont to dwell,
As the frail tenant shaped his growing shell,
Before thee lies revealed,—
Its irised ceiling rent, its sunless crypt unsealed!

Year after year beheld the silent toil
That spread his lustrous coil;
Still, as the spiral grew,
He left the past year's dwelling for the new,
Stole with soft step its shining archway through,
Built up its idle door,
Stretched in his last-found home, and knew the old no
    more.

Thanks for the heavenly message brought by thee,
Child of the wandering sea,

Cast from her lap, forlorn!
From thy dead lips a clearer note is born
Than ever Triton blew from wreathèd horn!
While on mine ear it rings,
Through the deep caves of thought I hear a voice that
　　sings:—

Build thee more stately mansions, O my soul,
As the swift seasons roll!
Leave thy low-vaulted past!
Let each new temple, nobler than the last,
Shut thee from heaven with a dome more vast,
Till thou at length art free,
Leaving thine outgrown shell by life's unresting sea!

OLIVER WENDELL HOLMES SR.

## Sea Fever

I must down to the seas again, to the lonely sea and the
    sky,
And all I ask is a tall ship and a star to steer her by;
And the wheel's kick and the wind's song and the white
    sail's shaking,
And a grey mist on the sea's face, and a grey dawn
    breaking.

I must down to the seas again, for the call of the running
    tide
Is a wild call and a clear call that may not be denied;
And all I ask is a windy day with the white clouds flying,
And the flung spray and the blown spume, and the sea-
    gulls crying.

I must down to the seas again, to the vagrant gypsy life,
To the gull's way and the whale's way where the wind's
    like a whetted knife;
And all I ask is a merry yarn from a laughing fellow-
    rover,
And quiet sleep and a sweet dream when the long trick's
    over.

JOHN MASEFIELD

## The Wreck of the Hesperus

It was the schooner Hesperus,
    That sailed the wintry sea;
And the skipper had taken his little daughtèr,
    To bear him company.

Blue were her eyes as the fairy-flax,
    Her cheeks like the dawn of day,
And her bosom white as the hawthorn buds,
    That ope in the month of May.

The skipper he stood beside the helm,
    His pipe was in his mouth,
And he watched how the veering flaw did blow
    The smoke now West, now South.

Then up and spake an old Sailòr,
    Had sailed to the Spanish Main,
"I pray thee, put into yonder port,
    For I fear a hurricane.

Last night, the moon had a golden ring,
    And to-night no moon we see!"
The skipper, he blew a whiff from his pipe,
    And a scornful laugh laughed he.

Colder and louder blew the wind,
    A gale from the Northeast,
The snow fell hissing in the brine,
    And the billows frothed like yeast.

Down came the storm, and smote amain
    The vessel in its strength;
She shuddered and paused, like a frighted steed,
    Then leaped her cable's length.

"Come hither! come hither! my little daughtèr,
    And do not tremble so;
For I can weather the roughest gale
    That ever wind did blow.

He wrapped her warm in his seaman's coat
    Against the stinging blast;
He cut a rope from a broken spar,
    And bound her to the mast.

"O father! I hear the church-bells ring,
    Oh say, what may it be?"
T is a fog-bell on a rock-bound coast! —
    And he steered for the open sea.

"O father! I hear the sound of guns,
    Oh say, what may it be?"
"Some ship in distress, that cannot live
    In such an angry sea!"

"O father! I see a gleaming light,
    Oh say, what may it be?"
But the father answered never a word,
    A frozen corpse was he.

Lashed to the helm, all stiff and stark,
    With his face turned to the skies,
The lantern gleamed through the gleaming snow
    On his fixed and glassy eyes.

Then the maiden clasped her hands and prayed
    That savèd she might be;
And she thought of Christ, who stilled the wave
    On the Lake of Galilee.

And fast through the midnight dark and drear,
    Through the whistling sleet and snow,
Like a sheeted ghost, the vessel swept
    Tow'rds the reef of Norman's Woe.

And ever the fitful gusts between
    A sound came from the land;
It was the sound of the trampling surf
    On the rocks and the hard sea-sand.

The breakers were right beneath her bows,
    She drifted a dreary wreck,
And a whooping billow swept the crew
    Like icicles from her deck.

She struck where the white and fleecy waves
    Looked soft as carded wool,
But the cruel rocks, they gored her side
    Like the horns of an angry bull.

Her rattling shrouds, all sheathed in ice,
    With the masts went by the board;
Like a vessel of glass, she stove and sank,
    Ho! ho! the breakers roared!

At daybreak, on the bleak sea-beach,
    A fisherman stood aghast,
To see the form of a maiden fair,
    Lashed close to a drifting mast.

The salt sea was frozen on her breast,
    The salt tears in her eyes;
And he saw her hair, like the brown sea-weed,
    On the billows fall and rise.

Such was the wreck of the Hesperus,
    In the midnight and the snow!
Christ save us all from a death like this,
    On the reef of Norman's Woe!

HENRY WADSWORTH LONGFELLOW

# The Castaway

Obscurest night involv'd the sky,
    Th' Atlantic billows roar'd,
When such a destin'd wretch as I,
    Wash'd headlong from on board,
Of friends, of hope, of all bereft,
His floating home for ever left.

No braver chief could Albion boast
    Than he with whom he went,
Nor ever ship left Albion's coast,
    With warmer wishes sent.
He lov'd them both, but both in vain,
Nor him beheld, nor her again.

Not long beneath the whelming brine,
    Expert to swim, he lay;
Nor soon he felt his strength decline,
    Or courage die away;
But wag'd with death a lasting strife,
Supported by despair of life.

He shouted: nor his friends had fail'd
    To check the vessel's course,
But so the furious blast prevail'd,
    That, pitiless perforce,
They left their outcast mate behind,
And scudded still before the wind.

Some succour yet they could afford;
    And, such as storms allow,
The cask, the coop, the floated cord,
    Delay'd not to bestow.
But he (they knew) nor ship, nor shore,
Whate'er they gave, should visit more.

Nor, cruel as it seem'd, could he
    Their haste himself condemn,
Aware that flight, in such a sea,
    Alone could rescue them;
Yet bitter felt it still to die
Deserted, and his friends so nigh.

He long survives, who lives an hour
    In ocean, self-upheld;
And so long he, with unspent pow'r,
    His destiny repell'd;
And ever, as the minutes flew,
Entreated help, or cried—Adieu!

At length, his transient respite past,
    His comrades, who before
Had heard his voice in ev'ry blast,
    Could catch the sound no more.
For then, by toil subdued, he drank
The stifling wave, and then he sank.

No poet wept him: but the page
    Of narrative sincere;
That tells his name, his worth, his age,
    Is wet with Anson's tear.
And tears by bards or heroes shed
Alike immortalize the dead.

I therefore purpose not, or dream,
    Descanting on his fate,
To give the melancholy theme
    A more enduring date:
But misery still delights to trace
  Its semblance in another's case.

No voice divine the storm allay'd,
    No light propitious shone;
When, snatch'd from all effectual aid,
    We perish'd, each alone:
But I beneath a rougher sea,
And whelm'd in deeper gulfs than he.

WILLIAM COWPER

## In the Wilderness

Mangled, uncared for, suffering thro' the night
　With heavenly patience the poor boy had lain;
Under the dreary shadows, left and right,
　Groaned on the wounded, stiffened out the slain.
　　What faith sustained his lone,
　　Brave heart to make no moan,
To send no cry from that blood-sprinkled sod,
Is a close mystery with him and God.

But when the light came, and the morning dew
　Glittered around him, like a golden lake,
And every dripping flower with deepened hue
　Looked through its tears for very pity's sake,
　　He moved his aching head
　　Upon his rugged bed,
And smiled as a blue violet, virgin-meek,
Laid her pure kiss upon his withered cheek.

At once there circled in his waking heart
　A thousand memories of distant home;
Of how those same blue violets would start
　Along his native fields, and some would roam
　　Down his dear humming brooks,
　　To hide in secret nooks,
And, shyly met, in nodding circles swing,
Like gossips murmuring at belated Spring.

And then he thought of the beloved hands
    That with his own had plucked the modest flower.
The blue-eyed maiden, crowned with golden bands,
    Who ruled as sovereign of that sunny hour.
      She at whose soft command
      He joined the mustering band,
She for whose sake he lay so firm and still,
Despite his pangs, not questioned then her will.

So, lost in thought, scarce conscious of the deed,
    Culling the violets, here and there he crept
Slowly—ah! slowly,—for his wound would bleed;
    And the sweet flowers themselves half smiled, half
        wept,
      To be thus gathered in
      By hands so pale and thin,
By fingers trembling as they neatly laid
Stem upon stem, and bound them in a braid.

The strangest posy ever fashioned yet
    Was clasped against the bosom of the lad,
As we, the seekers for the wounded, set
    His form upon our shoulders bowed and sad;
      Though he but seemed to think
      How violets nod and wink;
And as we cheered him, for the path was wild,
He only looked upon his flowers and smiled.

GEORGE HENRY BOKER

# The Pilgrim

*"Such a palmer ne'er was seene,*
*Lesse Love himselfe had palmer beene."*
*Never too late.*

Pilgrim feet, pray whither bound?
Pilgrim eyes, pray whither bent?
Sandal-shod and travel-gowned,
Lo, I seek the way they went
Late who passed toward Holy Land.

Pilgrim, it was long ago;
None remains who saw that band;
Grass and forest overgrow
Every path their footing wore.
Men are wise; they seek no more
Roads that lead to Holy Land.

Proud his look, as who should say:
I shall find where lies the way.

Pilgrim, thou art fair of face,
Staff and scrip are not for thee;
Gentle pilgrim, of thy grace,
Leave thy quest, and bide with me.
Love shall serve thee, joy shall bless;
Thou wert made for tenderness:
God's green world is fair and sweet;
Not o'er sea and Eastern strand,

But where friend and lover meet
Lies the way to Holy Land.

Low his voice, his lashes wet:
One day if God will—not yet.

Pilgrim, pardon me and heed.
Men of old who took that way
Went for fame of goodly deed,
Or, if sooth the stories say,
Sandalled priest, or knight in selle,
Flying each in pain and hate,
Harassed by stout fiends of hell,
Sought his crime to expiate.
Prithee, Pilgrim, go not hence;
Clear thy brow, and white thy hand,
What shouldst thou with penitence?
Wherefore seek to Holy Land?

Stern the whisper on his lip:
Sin and shame are in my scrip.

Pilgrim, pass, since it must be;
Take thy staff, and have thy will;
Prayer and love shall follow thee;
I will watch thee o'er the hill.
What thy fortune God doth know;
By what paths thy feet must go.
Far and dim the distance lies,
Yet my spirit prophesies:

Not in vigil lone and late,
Bowed upon the tropic sand,
But within the city gate,
In the struggle of the street,
Suddenly thine eyes shall meet
His whose look is Holy Land.

Smiled the pilgrim, sad and sage:
Long must be my pilgrimage.

SOPHIE JEWETT

# The Road and the End

I shall foot it
Down the roadway in the dusk,
Where shapes of hunger wander
And the fugitives of pain go by.

I shall foot it
In the silence of the morning,
See the night slur into dawn,
Hear the slow great winds arise
Where tall trees flank the way
And shoulder toward the sky.

The broken boulders by the road
Shall not commemorate my ruin.
Regret shall be the gravel under foot.
I shall watch for
Slim birds swift of wing
That go where wind and ranks of thunder
Drive the wild processionals of rain.

The dust of the travelled road
Shall touch my hands and face.

CARL SANDBURG

# The City of Sleep

Over the edge of the purple down,
  Where the single lamplight gleams,
Know ye the road to the Merciful Town
  That is hard by the Sea of Dreams –
Where the poor may lay their wrongs away,
  And the sick may forget to weep?
But we – pity us! Oh, pity us!
  We wakeful; ah, pity us! –
We must go back with Policeman Day –
  Back from the City of Sleep!

Weary they turn from the scroll and crown,
  Fetter and prayer and plough –
They that go up to the Merciful Town,
  For her gates are closing now.
It is their right in the Baths of Night
  Body and soul to steep,
But we – pity us! ah, pity us!
  We wakeful; oh, pity us! –
We must go back with Policeman Day –
  Back from the City of Sleep!

Over the edge of the purple down,
  Ere the tender dreams begin,
Look – we may look – at the Merciful Town,
  But we may not enter in!
Outcasts all, from her guarded wall
  Back to our watch we creep:

We – pity us! ah, pity us!
  We wakeful; ah, pity us! –
We that go back with Policeman Day –
  Back from the City of Sleep!

RUDYARD KIPLING

# Darkness

I had a dream, which was not all a dream.
The bright sun was extinguish'd, and the stars
Did wander darkling in the eternal space,
Rayless, and pathless, and the icy earth
Swung blind and blackening in the moonless air;
Morn came and went—and came, and brought no day,
And men forgot their passions in the dread
Of this their desolation; and all hearts
Were chill'd into a selfish prayer for light:
And they did live by watchfires—and the thrones,
The palaces of crowned kings—the huts,
The habitations of all things which dwell,
Were burnt for beacons; cities were consum'd,
And men were gather'd round their blazing homes
To look once more into each other's face;
Happy were those who dwelt within the eye
Of the volcanos, and their mountain-torch:
A fearful hope was all the world contain'd;
Forests were set on fire—but hour by hour
They fell and faded—and the crackling trunks
Extinguish'd with a crash—and all was black.
The brows of men by the despairing light
Wore an unearthly aspect, as by fits
The flashes fell upon them; some lay down
And hid their eyes and wept; and some did rest
Their chins upon their clenched hands, and smil'd;
And others hurried to and fro, and fed
Their funeral piles with fuel, and look'd up

With mad disquietude on the dull sky,
The pall of a past world; and then again
With curses cast them down upon the dust,
And gnash'd their teeth and howl'd: the wild birds
    shriek'd
And, terrified, did flutter on the ground,
And flap their useless wings; the wildest brutes
Came tame and tremulous; and vipers crawl'd
And twin'd themselves among the multitude,
Hissing, but stingless—they were slain for food.
And War, which for a moment was no more,
Did glut himself again: a meal was bought
With blood, and each sate sullenly apart
Gorging himself in gloom: no love was left;
All earth was but one thought—and that was death
Immediate and inglorious; and the pang
Of famine fed upon all entrails—men
Died, and their bones were tombless as their flesh;
The meagre by the meagre were devour'd,
Even dogs assail'd their masters, all save one,
And he was faithful to a corse, and kept
The birds and beasts and famish'd men at bay,
Till hunger clung them, or the dropping dead
Lur'd their lank jaws; himself sought out no food,
But with a piteous and perpetual moan,
And a quick desolate cry, licking the hand
Which answer'd not with a caress—he died.
The crowd was famish'd by degrees; but two
Of an enormous city did survive,
And they were enemies: they met beside

The dying embers of an altar-place
Where had been heap'd a mass of holy things
For an unholy usage; they rak'd up,
And shivering scrap'd with their cold skeleton hands
The feeble ashes, and their feeble breath
Blew for a little life, and made a flame
Which was a mockery; then they lifted up
Their eyes as it grew lighter, and beheld
Each other's aspects—saw, and shriek'd, and died—
Even of their mutual hideousness they died,
Unknowing who he was upon whose brow
Famine had written Fiend. The world was void,
The populous and the powerful was a lump,
Seasonless, herbless, treeless, manless, lifeless—
A lump of death—a chaos of hard clay.
The rivers, lakes and ocean all stood still,
And nothing stirr'd within their silent depths;
Ships sailorless lay rotting on the sea,
And their masts fell down piecemeal: as they dropp'd
They slept on the abyss without a surge—
The waves were dead; the tides were in their grave,
The moon, their mistress, had expir'd before;
The winds were wither'd in the stagnant air,
And the clouds perish'd; Darkness had no need
Of aid from them—She was the Universe.

LORD BYRON

## In Exile

Twilight is here, soft breezes bow the grass,
Day's sounds of various toil break slowly off.
The yoke-freed oxen low, the patient ass
Dips his dry nostril in the cool, deep trough.
Up from the prairie the tanned herdsmen pass
With frothy pails, guiding with voices rough
Their udder-lightened kine. Fresh smells of earth,
The rich, black furrows of the glebe send forth.

After the Southern day of heavy toil,
How good to lie, with limbs relaxed, brows bare
To evening's fan, and watch the smoke-wreaths coil
Up from one's pipe-stem through the rayless air.
So deem these unused tillers of the soil,
Who stretched beneath the shadowing oak tree, stare
Peacefully on the star-unfolding skies,
And name their life unbroken paradise.

The hounded stag that has escaped the pack,
And pants at ease within a thick-leaved dell;
The unimprisoned bird that finds the track
Through sun-bathed space, to where his fellows dwell;
The martyr, granted respite from the rack,
The death-doomed victim pardoned from his cell,—
Such only know the joy these exiles gain,—
Life's sharpest rapture is surcease of pain.

Strange faces theirs, wherethrough the Orient sun
Gleams from the eyes and glows athwart the skin.
Grave lines of studious thought and purpose run
From curl-crowned forehead to dark-bearded chin.
And over all the seal is stamped thereon
Of anguish branded by a world of sin,
In fire and blood through ages on their name,
Their seal of glory and the Gentiles' shame.

Freedom to love the law that Moses brought,
To sing the songs of David, and to think
The thoughts Gabirol to Spinoza taught,
Freedom to dig the common earth, to drink
The universal air—for this they sought
Refuge o'er wave and continent, to link
Egypt with Texas in their mystic chain,
And truth's perpetual lamp forbid to wane.

Hark! through the quiet evening air, their song
Floats forth with wild sweet rhythm and glad refrain.
They sing the conquest of the spirit strong,
The soul that wrests the victory from pain;
The noble joys of manhood that belong
To comrades and to brothers. In their strain
Rustle of palms and Eastern streams one hears,
And the broad prairie melts in mist of tears.

EMMA LAZARUS

## Consolation

Mist clogs the sunshine.
Smoky dwarf houses
Hem me round everywhere;
A vague dejection
Weighs down my soul.

Yet, while I languish,
Everywhere countless
Prospects unroll themselves,
And countless beings
Pass countless moods.

Far hence, in Asia,
On the smooth convent-roofs,
On the gilt terraces,
Of holy Lassa,
Bright shines the sun.

Grey time-worn marbles
Hold the pure Muses;
In their cool gallery,
By yellow Tiber,
They still look fair.

Strange unloved uproar
Shrills round their portal;
Yet not on Helicon
Kept they more cloudless
Their noble calm.

Through sun-proof alleys
In a lone, sand-hemm'd
City of Africa,
A blind, led beggar,
Age-bow'd, asks alms.

No bolder robber
Erst abode ambush'd
Deep in the sandy waste;
No clearer eyesight
Spied prey afar.

Saharan sand-winds
Sear'd his keen eyeballs;
Spent is the spoil he won.
For him the present
Holds only pain.

Two young, fair lovers,
Where the warm June-wind,
Fresh from the summer fields
Plays fondly round them,
Stand, tranced in joy.

With sweet, join'd voices,
And with eyes brimming:
Ah, they cry, "Destiny,
Prolong the present!
Time, stand still here!"

The prompt stern Goddess
Shakes her head, frowning;
Time gives his hour-glass
Its due reversal;
Their hour is gone.

With weak indulgence
Did the just Goddess
Lengthen their happiness,
She lengthen'd also
Distress elsewhere.

The hour, whose happy
Unalloy'd moments
I would eternalise,
Ten thousand mourners
Well pleased see end.

The bleak, stern hour,
Whose severe moments
I would annihilate,
Is pass'd by others
In warmth, light, joy.

Time, so complain'd of,
Who to no one man
Shows partiality,
Brings round to all men
Some undimm'd hours.

MATTHEW ARNOLD

## The Journey Onwards

As slow our ship her foamy track
 Against the wind was cleaving,
Her trembling pennant still look'd back
 To that dear isle 'twas leaving.
So loth we part from all we love,
 From all the links that bind us;
So turn our hearts, as on we rove,
 To those we've left behind us!

When, round the bowl, of vanish'd years
 We talk with joyous seeming—
With smiles that might as well be tears,
 So faint, so sad their beaming;
While memory brings us back again
 Each early tie that twined us,
Oh, sweet's the cup that circles then
 To those we've left behind us!

And when in other climes, we meet
 Some isle or vale enchanting,
Where all looks flowery wild and sweet,
 And nought but love is wanting;
We think how great had been our bliss
 If Heaven had but assign'd us
To live and die in scenes like this,
 With some we've left behind us!

As travellers oft look back at eve
 When eastward darkly going,
To gaze upon that light they leave
 Still faint behind them glowing,—
So, when the close of pleasure's day
 To gloom hath near consign'd us,
We turn to catch our fading ray
 Of joy that's left behind us.

THOMAS MOORE

# Part III

# Mother Nature

## Music

Sweet melody amidst the moving spheres
Breaks forth, a solemn and entrancing sound,
A harmony whereof the earth's green hills
Give but the faintest echo; yet is there
A music everywhere, and concert sweet!
All birds which sing amidst the forest deep
Till the flowers listen with unfolded bells;
All winds that murmur over summer grass,
Or curl the waves upon the pebbly shore;
Chiefly all earnest human voices rais'd
In charity and for the cause of truth,
Mingle together in one sacred chord,
And float, a grateful incense, up to God.

BESSIE RAYNER PARKES

## Nature

As a fond mother, when the day is o'er,
  Leads by the hand her little child to bed,
  Half willing, half reluctant to be led,
  And leave his broken playthings on the floor,
Still gazing at them through the open door,
  Nor wholly reassured and comforted
  By promises of others in their stead,
  Which, though more splendid, may not please him
    more;
So Nature deals with us, and takes away
  Our playthings one by one, and by the hand
  Leads us to rest so gently, that we go
Scarce knowing if we wish to go or stay,
  Being too full of sleep to understand
  How far the unknown transcends the what we know.

HENRY WADSWORTH LONGFELLOW

There is another Sky

There is another sky,
Ever serene and fair,
And there is another sunshine,
Though it be darkness there;
Never mind faded forests, Austin,
Never mind silent fields -
Here is a little forest,
Whose leaf is ever green;
Here is a brighter garden,
Where not a frost has been;
In its unfading flowers
I hear the bright bee hum:
Prithee, my brother,
Into my garden come!

EMILY DICKINSON

## On a Lane in Spring

A Little Lane, the brook runs close beside
And spangles in the sunshine while the fish glide swiftly
    by
And hedges leafing with the green spring tide
From out their greenery the old birds fly
And chirp and whistle in the morning sun
The pilewort glitters 'neath the pale blue sky
The little robin has its nest begun
And grass green linnets round the bushes fly
How Mild the Spring Comes in; the daisy buds
Lift up their golden blossoms to the sky
How lovely are the pingles and the woods
Here a beetle runs; and there a fly
Rests on the Arum leaf in bottle green
And all the Spring in this Sweet lane is seen

JOHN CLARE

# The Worship of Nature

The harp at Nature's advent strung
    Has never ceased to play;
The song the stars of morning sung
    Has never died away.

And prayer is made, and praise is given,
    By all things near and far;
The ocean looketh up to heaven,
    And mirrors every star.

Its waves are kneeling on the strand,
    As kneels the human knee,
Their white locks bowing to the sand,
    The priesthood of the sea!

They pour their glittering treasures forth,
    Their gifts of pearl they bring,
And all the listening hills of earth
    Take up the song they sing.

The green earth sends its incense up
    From many a mountain shrine;
From folded leaf and dewy cup
    She pours her sacred wine.

The mists above the morning rills
    Rise white as wings of prayer;
The altar-curtains of the hills
    Are sunset's purple air.

The winds with hymns of praise are loud,
    Or low with sobs of pain,—
The thunder-organ of the cloud,
    The dropping tears of rain.

With drooping head and branches crossed
    The twilight forest grieves,
Or speaks with tongues of Pentecost
    From all its sunlit leaves.

The blue sky is the temple's arch,
    Its transept earth and air,
The music of its starry march
    The chorus of a prayer.

So Nature keeps the reverent frame
    With which her years began,
And all her signs and voices shame
    The prayerless heart of man.

JOHN GREENLEAF WHITTIER

## A Light Exists in Spring

A Light exists in Spring
Not present on the Year
At any other period --
When March is scarcely here

A Color stands abroad
On Solitary Fields
That Science cannot overtake
But Human Nature feels.

It waits upon the Lawn,
It shows the furthest Tree
Upon the furthest Slope you know
It almost speaks to you.

Then as Horizons step
Or Noons report away
Without the Formula of sound
It passes and we stay --

A quality of loss
Affecting our Content
As Trade had suddenly encroached
Upon a Sacrament.

EMILY DICKINSON

## Song of Nature

Mine are the night and morning,
The pits of air, the gulf of space,
The sportive sun, the gibbous moon,
The innumerable days.

I hid in the solar glory,
I am dumb in the pealing song,
I rest on the pitch of the torrent,
In slumber I am strong.

No numbers have counted my tallies,
No tribes my house can fill,
I sit by the shining Fount of Life,
And pour the deluge still;

And ever by delicate powers
Gathering along the centuries
From race on race the rarest flowers,
My wreath shall nothing miss.

And many a thousand summers
My apples ripened well,
And light from meliorating stars
With firmer glory fell.

I wrote the past in characters
Of rock and fire the scroll,
The building in the coral sea,
The planting of the coal.

And thefts from satellites and rings
And broken stars I drew,
And out of spent and aged things
I formed the world anew;

What time the gods kept carnival,
Tricked out in star and flower,
And in cramp elf and saurian forms
They swathed their too much power.

Time and Thought were my surveyors,
They laid their courses well,
They boiled the sea, and baked the layers
Or granite, marl, and shell.

But he, the man-child glorious,--
Where tarries he the while?
The rainbow shines his harbinger,
The sunset gleams his smile.

My boreal lights leap upward,
Forthright my planets roll,
And still the man-child is not born,
The summit of the whole.

Must time and tide forever run?
Will never my winds go sleep in the west?
Will never my wheels which whirl the sun
And satellites have rest?

Too much of donning and doffing,
Too slow the rainbow fades,
I weary of my robe of snow,
My leaves and my cascades;

I tire of globes and races,
Too long the game is played;
What without him is summer's pomp,
Or winter's frozen shade?

I travail in pain for him,
My creatures travail and wait;
His couriers come by squadrons,
He comes not to the gate.

Twice I have moulded an image,
And thrice outstretched my hand,
Made one of day, and one of night,
And one of the salt sea-sand.

One in a Judaean manger,
And one by Avon stream,
One over against the mouths of Nile,
And one in the Academe.

I moulded kings and saviours,
And bards o'er kings to rule;--
But fell the starry influence short,
The cup was never full.

Yet whirl the glowing wheels once more,
And mix the bowl again;
Seethe, fate! the ancient elements,
Heat, cold, wet, dry, and peace, and pain.

Let war and trade and creeds and song
Blend, ripen race on race,
The sunburnt world a man shall breed
Of all the zones, and countless days.

No ray is dimmed, no atom worn,
My oldest force is good as new,
And the fresh rose on yonder thorn
Gives back the bending heavens in dew.

RALPH WALDO EMERSON

# Spring

To what purpose, April, do you return again?
Beauty is not enough.
You can no longer quiet me with the redness
Of little leaves opening stickily.
I know what I know.
The sun is hot on my neck as I observe
The spikes of the crocus.
The smell of the earth is good.
It is apparent that there is no death.
But what does that signify?
Not only under ground are the brains of men
Eaten by maggots.
Life in itself
Is nothing,
An empty cup, a flight of uncarpeted stairs.
It is not enough that yearly, down this hill,
April
Comes like an idiot, babbling and strewing flowers

EDNA ST. VINCENT MILLAY

# A Bird Came down the Walk

A bird came down the walk:
He did not know I saw;
He bit an angle-worm in halves
And ate the fellow, raw.

And then he drank a dew
From a convenient grass,
And then hopped sidewise to the wall
To let a beetle pass.

He glanced with rapid eyes
That hurried all abroad,--
They looked like frightened beads, I thought;
He stirred his velvet head

Like one in danger; cautious,
I offered him a crumb,
And he unrolled his feathers
And rowed him softer home

Than oars divide the ocean,
Too silver for a seam,
Or butterflies, off banks of noon,
Leap, plashless, as they swim.

EMILY DICKINSON

# Birches

When I see birches bend to left and right
Across the lines of straighter darker trees,
I like to think some boy's been swinging them.
But swinging doesn't bend them down to stay
As ice-storms do. Often you must have seen them
Loaded with ice a sunny winter morning
After a rain. They click upon themselves
As the breeze rises, and turn many-colored
As the stir cracks and crazes their enamel.
Soon the sun's warmth makes them shed crystal shells
Shattering and avalanching on the snow-crust--
Such heaps of broken glass to sweep away
You'd think the inner dome of heaven had fallen.
They are dragged to the withered bracken by the load,
And they seem not to break; though once they are
    bowed
So low for long, they never right themselves:
You may see their trunks arching in the woods
Years afterwards, trailing their leaves on the ground
Like girls on hands and knees that throw their hair
Before them over their heads to dry in the sun.
But I was going to say when Truth broke in
With all her matter-of-fact about the ice-storm
I should prefer to have some boy bend them
As he went out and in to fetch the cows--
Some boy too far from town to learn baseball,
Whose only play was what he found himself,
Summer or winter, and could play alone.

One by one he subdued his father's trees
By riding them down over and over again
Until he took the stiffness out of them,
And not one but hung limp, not one was left
For him to conquer. He learned all there was
To learn about not launching out too soon
And so not carrying the tree away
Clear to the ground. He always kept his poise
To the top branches, climbing carefully
With the same pains you use to fill a cup
Up to the brim, and even above the brim.
Then he flung outward, feet first, with a swish,
Kicking his way down through the air to the ground.
So was I once myself a swinger of birches.
And so I dream of going back to be.
It's when I'm weary of considerations,
And life is too much like a pathless wood
Where your face burns and tickles with the cobwebs
Broken across it, and one eye is weeping
From a twig's having lashed across it open.
I'd like to get away from earth awhile
And then come back to it and begin over.
May no fate willfully misunderstand me
And half grant what I wish and snatch me away
Not to return. Earth's the right place for love:
I don't know where it's likely to go better.
I'd like to go by climbing a birch tree,
And climb black branches up a snow-white trunk
Toward heaven, till the tree could bear no more,
But dipped its top and set me down again.

That would be good both going and coming back.
One could do worse than be a swinger of birches.

ROBERT FROST

# The Fish

I caught a tremendous fish
and held him beside the boat
half out of water, with my hook
fast in a corner of his mouth.
He didn't fight.
He hadn't fought at all.
He hung a grunting weight,
battered and venerable
and homely. Here and there
his brown skin hung in strips
like ancient wallpaper,
and its pattern of darker brown
was like wallpaper:
shapes like full-blown roses
stained and lost through age.
He was speckled with barnacles,
fine rosettes of lime,
and infested
with tiny white sea-lice,
and underneath two or three
rags of green weed hung down.
While his gills were breathing in
the terrible oxygen
—the frightening gills,
fresh and crisp with blood,
that can cut so badly—
I thought of the coarse white flesh
packed in like feathers,

the big bones and the little bones,
the dramatic reds and blacks
of his shiny entrails,
and the pink swim-bladder
like a big peony.
I looked into his eyes
which were far larger than mine
but shallower, and yellowed,
the irises backed and packed
with tarnished tinfoil
seen through the lenses
of old scratched isinglass.
They shifted a little, but not
to return my stare.
—It was more like the tipping
of an object toward the light.
I admired his sullen face,
the mechanism of his jaw,
and then I saw
that from his lower lip
—if you could call it a lip—
grim, wet, and weaponlike,
hung five old pieces of fish-line,
or four and a wire leader
with the swivel still attached,
with all their five big hooks
grown firmly in his mouth.
A green line, frayed at the end
where he broke it, two heavier lines,
and a fine black thread

still crimped from the strain and snap
when it broke and he got away.
Like medals with their ribbons
frayed and wavering,
a five-haired beard of wisdom
trailing from his aching jaw.
I stared and stared
and victory filled up
the little rented boat,
from the pool of bilge
where oil had spread a rainbow
around the rusted engine
to the bailer rusted orange,
the sun-cracked thwarts,
the oarlocks on their strings,
the gunnels—until everything
was rainbow, rainbow, rainbow!
And I let the fish go.

ELIZABETH BISHOP

## Memory

My mind lets go a thousand things
Like dates of wars and deaths of kings,
And yet recalls the very hour--
T was noon by yonder village tower,
And on the last blue noon in May--
The wind came briskly up this way,
Crisping the brook beside the road;
Then, pausing here, set down its load
Of pine-scents, and shook listlessly
Two petals from that wild-rose tree.

THOMAS BAILEY ALDRICH

# The Education of Nature

Three years she grew in sun and shower;
Then Nature said, "A lovelier flower
On earth was never sown;
This child I to myself will take;
She shall be mine, and I will make
A lady of my own.

"Myself will to my darling be
Both law and impulse: and with me
The girl, in rock and plain,
In earth and heaven, in glade and bower
Shall feel an overseeing power
To kindle or restrain.

"She shall be sportive as the fawn
That wild with glee across the lawn
Or up the mountain springs;
And her's shall be the breathing balm,
And her's the silence and the calm
Of mute insensate things.

"The floating clouds their state shall lend
To her; for her the willow bend;
Nor shall she fail to see
E'en in the motions of the storm
Grace that shall mould the maiden's form
By silent sympathy.

"The stars of midnight shall be dear
To her; and she shall lean her ear
In many a secret place
Where rivulets dance their wayward round,
And beauty born of murmuring sound
Shall pass into her face.

"And vital feelings of delight
Shall rear her form to stately height,
Her virgin bosom swell;
Such thoughts to Lucy I will give
While she and I together live
Here in this happy dell."

Thus Nature spake—The work was done—
How soon my Lucy's race was run!
She died, and left to me
This heath, this calm and quiet scene;
The memory of what has been,
And never more will be.

WILLIAM WORDSWORTH

## The Eagle

He clasps the crag with crooked hands;
Close to the sun in lonely lands,
Ringed with the azure world, he stands.

The wrinkled sea beneath him crawls;
He watches from his mountain walls,
And like a thunderbolt he falls.

LORD TENNYSON

## The Soote Season

The soote season, that bud and bloom forth brings
With green hath clad the hill and eke the vale;
The nightingale with feathers new she sings;
And turtle to her make hath told her tale.
Summer is come, for every spray now springs;
The hart hath hung his old head on the pale;
The buck in brake his winter coat he flings;
The fishes flete with new repairèd scale;
The adder all her slough away she slings;
The swift swalllow pursueth the flies small;
The busy bee her honey now she mings;
Winter is worn that was the flowers' bale.
And thus I see among these pleasant things
Each care decays, and yet my sorrow springs.

HENRY HOWARD, EARL OF SURREY

# Thoughts in a Garden

How vainly men themselves amaze
To win the palm, the oak, or bays,
And their incessant labours see
Crown'd from some single herb or tree,
Whose short and narrow-vergéd shade
Does prudently their toils upbraid;
While all the flowers and trees do close
To weave the garlands of Repose.

Fair Quiet, have I found thee here,
And Innocence thy sister dear?
Mistaken long, I sought you then
In busy companies of men:
Your sacred plants, if here below,
Only among the plants will grow:
Society is all but rude
To this delicious solitude.

No white nor red was ever seen
So amorous as this lovely green.
Fond lovers, cruel as their flame,
Cut in these trees their mistress' name:
Little, alas! they know or heed
How far these beauties hers exceed!
Fair trees! where'er your barks I wound,
No name shall but your own be found.

When we have run our passions' heat,
Love hither makes his best retreat:
The gods, who mortal beauty chase,
Still in a tree did end their race:
Apollo hunted Daphne so
Only that she might laurel grow;
And Pan did after Syrinx speed
Not as a nymph, but for a reed.

What wondrous life in this I lead!
Ripe apples drop about my head;
The luscious clusters of the vine
Upon my mouth do crush their wine;
The nectarine and curious peach
Into my hands themselves do reach;
Stumbling on melons, as I pass,
Ensnared with flowers, I fall on grass.

Meanwhile the mind from pleasure less
Withdraws into its happiness;
The mind, that ocean where each kind
Does straight its own resemblance find;
Yet it creates, transcending these,
Far other worlds, and other seas;
Annihilating all that's made
To a green thought in a green shade.

Here at the fountain's sliding foot
Or at some fruit-tree's mossy root,

Casting the body's vest aside
My soul into the boughs does glide;
There, like a bird, it sits and sings,
Then whets and claps its silver wings,
And, till prepared for longer flight,
Waves in its plumes the various light.

Such was that happy Garden-state
While man there walk'd without a mate:
After a place so pure and sweet,
What other help could yet be meet!
But 'twas beyond a mortal's share
To wander solitary there:
Two paradises are in one,
To live in Paradise alone.

How well the skilful gardener drew
Of flowers and herbs this dial new!
Where, from above, the milder sun
Does through a fragrant zodiac run:
And, as it works, th' industrious bee
Computes its time as well as we.
How could such sweet and wholesome hours
Be reckon'd, but with herbs and flowers!

ANDREW MARVELL

# A Minor Bird

I have wished a bird would fly away,
And not sing by my house all day;

Have clapped my hands at him from the door
When it seemed as if I could bear no more.

The fault must partly have been in me.
The bird was not to blame for his key.

And of course there must be something wrong
In wanting to silence any song.

ROBERT FROST

# God the Artist

God, when you thought of a pine tree,
How did you think of a star?
How did you dream of the Milky Way
To guide us from afar.
How did you think of a clean brown pool
Where flecks of shadows are?

God, when you thought of a cobweb,
How did you think of dew?
How did you know a spider's house
Had shingles bright and new?
How did you know the human folk
Would love them like they do?

God, when you patterned a bird song,
Flung on a silver string,
How did you know the ecstasy
That crystal call would bring?
How did you think of a bubbling throat
And a darling speckled wing?

God, when you chiseled a raindrop,
How did you think of a stem,
Bearing a lovely satin leaf
To hold the tiny gem?
How did you know a million drops
Would deck the morning's hem?

Why did you mate the moonlit night
With the honeysuckle vines?
How did you know Madeira bloom
Distilled ecstatic wines?
How did you weave the velvet disk
Where tangled perfumes are?
God, when you thought of a pine tree,
How did you think of a star?

ANGELA MORGAN

## Leisure

What is this life if, full of care,
We have no time to stand and stare?—

No time to stand beneath the boughs,
And stare as long as sheep and cows:

No time to see, when woods we pass,
Where squirrels hide their nuts in grass:

No time to see, in broad daylight,
Streams full of stars, like skies at night:

No time to turn at Beauty's glance,
And watch her feet, how they can dance:

No time to wait till her mouth can
Enrich that smile her eyes began?

A poor life this if, full of care,
We have no time to stand and stare.

WILLIAM HENRY DAVIES

## A Kind of Paradise

Walking through the mango trees, the horses
are there, throats taut like plucked strings
as they suck cool water from the basin.
The bay stomps a foot. Her moony rump heaves,
and so the day exhales. No air sweeter than here,
no light more golden, the warmth of that light
held by the mangoes long after dusk has muscled
in. This privacy between horizons, the weightless
silence. Fruit drops clean through air into soil.
The reliability of that. The horses swing their heads
to spit the punctured skins back into earth.
In the flimmering night the canopy resembles
something impenetrable. How ancient this all is.
To lie among the trees and hear the horses
breathe under a black sky, the ground sweet
with rotten fruit. Managing desires as they come,
little by little: food, water, sleep. Love, even.
Understanding this as the happiness
the horses know, between the trees in summer.

MINDY GILL

# Peace

The steadfast coursing of the stars,
The waves that ripple to the shore,
The vigorous trees which year by year
Spread upwards more and more;

The jewel forming in the mine,
The snow that falls so soft and light,
The rising and the setting sun,
The growing glooms of night;

All natural things both live and move
In natural peace that is their own;
Only in our disordered life
Almost is she unknown.

She is not rest, nor sleep, nor death;
Order and motion ever stand
To carry out her firm behests
As guards at her right hand.

And something of her living force
Fashions the lips when Christians say
To Him Whose strength sustains the world,
"Give us Thy Peace, we pray!"

BESSIE RAYNER PARKES

## The Noble Nature

It is not growing like a tree
  In bulk, doth make Man better be;
Or standing long an oak, three hundred year,
To fall a log at last, dry, bald, and sere:
  A lily of a day
  Is fairer far in May,
  Although it fall and die that night—
  It was the plant and flower of Light.
In small proportions we just beauties see;
And in short measures life may perfect be.

BENJAMIN JONSON

## Fog

Like bodiless water passing in a sigh,
Thro' palsied streets the fatal shadows flow,
And in their sharp disastrous undertow
Suck in the morning sun, and all the sky.
The towery vista sinks upon the eye,
As if it heard the Hebrew bugles blow,
Black and dissolved; nor could the founders know
How what was built so bright should daily die.

Thy mood with man's is broken and blent in,
City of Stains! And ache of thought doth drown
The primitive light in which thy life began;
Great as thy dole is, smirchèd with his sin,
Greater and elder yet the love of man
Full in thy look, tho' the dark visor's down.

LOUISE IMOGEN GUINEY

# My November Guest

My Sorrow, when she's here with me,
Thinks these dark days of autumn rain
Are beautiful as days can be;
She loves the bare, the withered tree;
She walks the sodden pasture lane.

Her pleasure will not let me stay.
She talks and I am fain to list:
She's glad the birds are gone away,
She's glad her simple worsted grey
Is silver now with clinging mist.

The desolate, deserted trees,
The faded earth, the heavy sky,
The beauties she so truly sees,
She thinks I have no eye for these,
And vexes me for reason why.

Not yesterday I learned to know
The love of bare November days
Before the coming of the snow,
But it were vain to tell her so,
And they are better for her praise.

ROBERT FROST

## To Autumn

Season of mists and mellow fruitfulness,
Close bosom-friend of the maturing sun;
Conspiring with him how to load and bless
With fruit the vines that round the thatch-eves run;
To bend with apples the moss'd cottage-trees,
And fill all fruit with ripeness to the core;
To swell the gourd, and plump the hazel shells
With a sweet kernel; to set budding more,
And still more, later flowers for the bees,
Until they think warm days will never cease,
For summer has o'er-brimm'd their clammy cells.

Who hath not seen thee oft amid thy store?
Sometimes whoever seeks abroad may find
Thee sitting careless on a granary floor,
Thy hair soft-lifted by the winnowing wind;
Or on a half-reap'd furrow sound asleep,
Drows'd with the fume of poppies, while thy hook
Spares the next swath and all its twined flowers:
And sometimes like a gleaner thou dost keep
Steady thy laden head across a brook;
Or by a cyder-press, with patient look,
Thou watchest the last oozings hours by hours.

Where are the songs of spring? Ay, Where are they?
Think not of them, thou hast thy music too,--
While barred clouds bloom the soft-dying day,
And touch the stubble-plains with rosy hue;
Then in a wailful choir the small gnats mourn
Among the river sallows, borne aloft
Or sinking as the light wind lives or dies;
And full-grown lambs loud bleat from hilly bourn;
Hedge-crickets sing; and now with treble soft
The red-breast whistles from a garden-croft;
And gathering swallows twitter in the skies.

JOHN KEATS

## Nothing Gold Can Stay

Nature's first green is gold,
Her hardest hue to hold.
Her early leaf's a flower;
But only so an hour.
Then leaf subsides to leaf.
So Eden sank to grief,
So dawn goes down to day.
Nothing gold can stay.

ROBERT FROST

## Tell Me Not Here, It Needs Not Saying

Tell me not here, it needs not saying,
What tune the enchantress plays
In aftermaths of soft September
Or under blanching mays,
For she and I were long acquainted
And I knew all her ways.

On russet floors, by waters idle,
The pine lets fall its cone;
The cuckoo shouts all day at nothing
In leafy dells alone;
And traveller's joy beguiles in autumn
Hearts that have lost their own.

On acres of the seeded grasses
The changing burnish heaves;
Or marshalled under moons of harvest
Stand still all night the sheaves;
Or beeches strip in storms for winter
And stain the wind with leaves.

Possess, as I possessed a season,
The countries I resign,
Where over elmy plains the highway
Would mount the hills and shine,
And full of shade the pillared forest
Would murmur and be mine.

For nature, heartless, witless nature,
Will neither care nor know
What stranger's feet may find the meadow
And trespass there and go,
Nor ask amid the dews of morning
If they are mine or no.

ALFRED EDWARD HOUSMAN

## The Lessons of Nature

Of this fair volume which we World do name
If we the sheets and leaves could turn with care,
Of Him who it corrects, and did it frame,
We clear might read the art and wisdom rare:

Find out His power which wildest powers doth tame,
His providence extending everywhere,
His justice which proud rebels doth not spare,
In every page, no period of the same.

But silly we, like foolish children, rest
Well pleased with colour'd vellum, leaves of gold,
Fair dangling ribbands, leaving what is best,
On the great Writer's sense ne'er taking hold;

Or if by chance we stay our minds on aught,
It is some picture on the margin wrought.

WILLIAM DRUMMOND

## Pray to what Earth

Pray to what earth does this sweet cold belong,
Which asks no duties and no conscience?
The moon goes up by leaps, her cheerful path
In some far summer stratum of the sky,
While stars with their cold shine bedot her way.
The fields gleam mildly back upon the sky,
And far and near upon the leafless shrubs
The snow dust still emits a silver light.
Under the hedge, where drift banks are their screen,
The titmice now pursue their downy dreams,
As often in the sweltering summer nights
The bee doth drop asleep in the flower cup,
When evening overtakes him with his load.
By the brooksides, in the still, genial night,
The more adventurous wanderer may hear
The crystals shoot and form, and winter slow
Increase his rule by gentlest summer means

HENRY DAVID THOREAU

## Desert Places

Snow falling and night falling fast, oh, fast
In a field I looked into going past,
And the ground almost covered smooth in snow,
But a few weeds and stubble showing last.

The woods around it have it--it is theirs.
All animals are smothered in their lairs.
I am too absent-spirited to count;
The loneliness includes me unawares.

And lonely as it is that loneliness
Will be more lonely ere it will be less--
A blanker whiteness of benighted snow
With no expression, nothing to express.

They cannot scare me with their empty spaces
Between stars--on stars where no human race is.
I have it in me so much nearer home
To scare myself with my own desert places.

ROBERT FROST

## No Songs in Winter

The sky is gray as gray may be,
There is no bird upon the bough,
There is no leaf on vine or tree.

In the Neponset marshes now
Willow-stems, rosy in the wind,
Shiver with hidden sense of snow.

So too 't is winter in my mind,
No light-winged fancy comes and stays:
A season churlish and unkind.

Slow creep the hours, slow creep the days,
The black ink crusts upon the pen--
Just wait till bluebirds, wrens, and jays
And golden orioles come again!

THOMAS BAILEY ALDRICH

## February Twilight

I stood beside a hill
Smooth with new-laid snow,
A single star looked out
From the cold evening glow.

There was no other creature
That saw what I could see—
I stood and watched the evening star
As long as it watched me.

SARA TEASDALE

# A Winter Blue Jay

Crisply the bright snow whispered,
Crunching beneath our feet;
Behind us as we walked along the parkway,
Our shadows danced,
Fantastic shapes in vivid blue.
Across the lake the skaters
Flew to and fro,
With sharp turns weaving
A frail invisible net.
In ecstasy the earth
Drank the silver sunlight;
In ecstasy the skaters
Drank the wine of speed;
In ecstasy we laughed
Drinking the wine of love.
Had not the music of our joy
Sounded its highest note?
But no,
For suddenly, with lifted eyes you said,
"Oh look!"
There, on the black bough of a snow flecked maple,
Fearless and gay as our love,
A bluejay cocked his crest!
Oh who can tell the range of joy
Or set the bounds of beauty?

SARA TEASDALE

## Stopping by Woods on a Snowy Evening

Whose woods these are I think I know.
His house is in the village though;
He will not see me stopping here
To watch his woods fill up with snow.

My little horse must think it queer
To stop without a farmhouse near
Between the woods and frozen lake
The darkest evening of the year.

He gives his harness bells a shake
To ask if there is some mistake.
The only other sound's the sweep
Of easy wind and downy flake.

The woods are lovely, dark and deep,
But I have promises to keep,
And miles to go before I sleep,
And miles to go before I sleep.

ROBERT FROST

# The Way through the Woods

They shut the road through the woods
  Seventy years ago.
Weather and rain have undone it again,
  And now you would never know
There was once a path through the woods
  Before they planted the trees:
It is underneath the coppice and heath,
  And the thin anemones.
  Only the keeper sees
That, where the ring-dove broods
  And the badgers roll at ease,
There was once a road through the woods.

Yet, if you enter the woods
  Of a summer evening late,
When the night-air cools on the trout-ring'd pools
  Where the otter whistles his mate
(They fear not men in the woods
  Because they see so few),
You will hear the beat of a horse's feet
  And the swish of a skirt in the dew,
  Steadily cantering through
The misty solitudes,
  As though they perfectly knew
The old lost road through the woods ...
But there is no road through the woods.

RUDYARD KIPLING

## The Darkling Thrush

I leant upon a coppice gate
   When Frost was spectre-gray,
And Winter's dregs made desolate
   The weakening eye of day.
The tangled bine-stems scored the sky
   Like strings of broken lyres,
And all mankind that haunted nigh
   Had sought their household fires.

The land's sharp features seemed to be
   The Century's corpse outleant,
His crypt the cloudy canopy,
   The wind his death-lament.
The ancient pulse of germ and birth
   Was shrunken hard and dry,
And every spirit upon earth
   Seemed fervourless as I.

At once a voice arose among
   The bleak twigs overhead
In a full-hearted evensong
   Of joy illimited;
An aged thrush, frail, gaunt, and small,
   In blast-beruffled plume,
Had chosen thus to fling his soul
   Upon the growing gloom.

So little cause for carolings
   Of such ecstatic sound
Was written on terrestrial things
   Afar or nigh around,
That I could think there trembled through
   His happy good-night air
Some blessed Hope, whereof he knew
   And I was unaware.

THOMAS HARDY

## Thaw

Over the land freckled with snow half-thawed
The speculating rooks at their nests cawed
And saw from elm-tops, delicate as flowers of grass,
What we below could not see, Winter pass.

EDWARD THOMAS

# Part IV

# Passion

## She Walks in Beauty

She walks in beauty, like the night
Of cloudless climes and starry skies;
And all that's best of dark and bright
Meet in her aspect and her eyes:
Thus mellowed to that tender light
Which heaven to gaudy day denies.

One shade the more, one ray the less,
Had half impaired the nameless grace
Which waves in every raven tress,
Or softly lightens o'er her face;
Where thoughts serenely sweet express
How pure, how dear their dwelling place.

And on that cheek, and o'er that brow,
So soft, so calm, yet eloquent,
The smiles that win, the tints that glow,
But tell of days in goodness spent,
A mind at peace with all below,
A heart whose love is innocent!

LORD BYRON

# When I Too Long Have Looked Upon Your Face

When I too long have looked upon your face,
Wherein for me a brightness unobscured
Save by the mists of brightness has its place,
And terrible beauty not to be endured,
I turn away reluctant from your light,
And stand irresolute, a mind undone,
A silly, dazzled thing deprived of sight
From having looked too long upon the sun.
Then is my daily life a narrow room
In which a little while, uncertainly,
Surrounded by impenetrable gloom,
Among familiar things grown strange to me
Making my way, I pause, and feel, and hark,
Till I become accustomed to the dark.

EDNA ST. VINCENT MILLAY

# Echo

Come to me in the silence of the night;
  Come in the speaking silence of a dream;
Come with soft rounded cheeks and eyes as bright
  As sunlight on a stream;
    Come back in tears,
O memory, hope, love of finished years.

Oh dream how sweet, too sweet, too bitter sweet,
  Whose wakening should have been in Paradise,
Where souls brimfull of love abide and meet;
  Where thirsting longing eyes
    Watch the slow door
That opening, letting in, lets out no more.

Yet come to me in dreams, that I may live
  My very life again tho' cold in death:
Come back to me in dreams, that I may give
  Pulse for pulse, breath for breath:
    Speak low, lean low,
As long ago, my love, how long ago.

CHRISTINA ROSSETTI

# She Was a Phantom of Delight

She was a Phantom of delight
When first she gleamed upon my sight;
A lovely Apparition, sent
To be a moment's ornament;
Her eyes as stars of Twilight fair;
Like Twilight's, too, her dusky hair;
But all things else about her drawn
From May-time and the cheerful Dawn;
A dancing Shape, an Image gay,
To haunt, to startle, and way-lay.
I saw her upon nearer view,
A Spirit, yet a Woman too!
Her household motions light and free,
And steps of virgin-liberty;
A countenance in which did meet
Sweet records, promises as sweet;
A Creature not too bright or good
For human nature's daily food;
For transient sorrows, simple wiles,
Praise, blame, love, kisses, tears, and smiles.
And now I see with eye serene
The very pulse of the machine;
A Being breathing thoughtful breath,
A Traveller between life and death;
The reason firm, the temperate will,
Endurance, foresight, strength, and skill;
A perfect Woman, nobly planned,
To warn, to comfort, and command;

And yet a Spirit still, and bright
With something of angelic light.

WILLIAM WORDSWORTH

# Revelation

Into the silver night
    She brought with her pale hand
  The topaz lanthorn-light,
And darted splendour o'er the land;
    Around her in a band,
Ringstraked and pied, the great soft moths came flying,
  And flapping with their mad wings, fann'd
The flickering flame, ascending, falling, dying.

Behind the thorny pink
    Close wall of blossom'd may,
  I gazed thro' one green chink
And saw no more than thousands may,—
    Saw sweetness, tender and gay,—
Saw full rose lips as rounded as the cherry,
  Saw braided locks more dark than bay,
And flashing eyes decorous, pure, and merry.

With food for furry friends
    She pass'd, her lamp and she,
  Till eaves and gable-ends
Hid all that saffron sheen from me:
    Around my rosy tree
Once more the silver-starry night was shining,
  With depths of heaven, dewy and free,
And crystals of a carven moon declining.

Alas! for him who dwells
    In frigid air of thought,
  When warmer light dispels
The frozen calm his spirit sought;
    By life too lately taught
He sees the ecstatic Human from him stealing;
  Reels from the joy experience brought,
And dares not clutch what Love was half revealing.

SIR EDMUND GOSSE

## The True Beauty

He that loves a rosy cheek
 Or a coral lip admires,
Or from star-like eyes doth seek
 Fuel to maintain his fires;
As old Time makes these decay,
So his flames must waste away.

But a smooth and steadfast mind,
 Gentle thoughts, and calm desires,
Hearts with equal love combined,
 Kindle never-dying fires:—
Where these are not, I despise
Lovely cheeks or lips or eyes.

T. CAREW

## Surrender

Doubt me, my dim companion!
Why, God would be content
With but a fraction of the love
Poured thee without a stint.

The whole of me, forever,
What more the woman can, --
Say quick, that I may dower thee
With last delight I own!

It cannot be my spirit,
For that was thine before;
I ceded all of dust I knew, --
What opulence the more

Had I, a humble maiden,
Whose farthest of degree
Was that she might,
Some distant heaven,
Dwell timidly with thee!

EMILY DICKINSON

# Know Me in This Moment

*A poem to those beautiful, generous people who accept others, giving a warm hug to those in need.*

A city of lights,
shining in every corner,
full of love, within hearts,
blooming in the atmosphere.

A city of vivid dreams,
a dream to become a proud father or a mother as royal
    as a queen,
a prosperous businessman, a teacher,
teaching humanity
or a doctor,
saving lives.

A city of life,
of inspiration,
of hope and enthusiasm,
my city, the city of dreams
today is dead!

As darkness blew out our lights,
and tears became our lows,
and death sacrificed our love,
blood became the only colour of life,

A city of death,
of discourage,
of fear and collapse
has written my story of survival,

I come from disaster, from null, from nadir!
I sit in your land, beside your flowers,
asking for a feeling,
know me as you are.

Know me in this same moment,
in the fear in your eyes,
the break in your heart,
the torture in your life,

Tell me,
Have you ever forgotten your being?
your dreams?
forgotten your details?
your identity
forgotten your presence?
your breathing?

I had no choice,

When it's me in your presence,
we're both a soul!

I open my eyes,
I survived, I am alive!

I breathe, I am myself!
A beating heart, running thought,
A hot warm blood reason to go ahead!

Hope is here, future is enough,
We are enough!

Take my hands, raise me up,
I offer you love,

can you offer the same?

HADISE ANSARI

# At Last

At last, when all the summer shine
That warmed life's early hours is past,
Your loving fingers seek for mine
And hold them close-at last-at last!
Not oft the robin comes to build
Its nest upon the leafless bough
By autumn robbed, by winter chilled,
But you, dear heart, you love me now.

Though there are shadows on my brow
And furrows on my cheek, in truth,
The marks where Time's remorseless plough
Broke up the blooming sward of Youth,
Though fled is every girlish grace
Might win or hold a lover's vow,
Despite my sad and faded face,
And darkened heart, you love me now!

I count no more my wasted tears;
They left no echo of their fall;
I mourn no more my lonesome years;
This blessed hour atones for all.
I fear not all that Time or Fate
May bring to burden heart or brow,
Strong in the love that came so late,
Our souls shall keep it always now!

ELIZABETH AKERS ALLEN

## To the Evening Star

Gem of the crimson-colour'd Even,
Companion of retiring day,
Why at the closing gates of heaven,
Beloved Star, dost thou delay?

So fair thy pensile beauty burns
When soft the tear of twilight flows;
So due thy plighted love returns
To chambers brighter than the rose;

To Peace, to Pleasure, and to love
So kind a star thou seem'st to be,
Sure some enamour'd orb above
Descends and burns to meet with thee.

Thine is the breathing, blushing hour
When all unheavenly passions fly,
Chased by the soul-subduing power
Of Love's delicious witchery.

O! sacred to the fall of day
Queen of propitious stars, appear,
And early rise, and long delay
When Caroline herself is here!

Shine on her chosen green resort
Whose trees the sunward summit crown,
And wanton flowers, that well may court
An angel's feet to tread them down:—

Shine on her sweetly scented road
Thou star of evening's purple dome,
That lead'st the nightingale abroad,
And guid'st the pilgrim to his home.

Shine where my charmer's sweeter breath
Embalms the soft exhaling dew,
Where dying winds a sigh bequeath
To kiss the cheek of rosy hue:—

Where, winnow'd by the gentle air,
Her silken tresses darkly flow
And fall upon her brow so fair,
Like shadows on the mountain snow.

Thus, ever thus, at day's decline
In converse sweet to wander far—
O bring with thee my Caroline,
And thou shalt be my Ruling Star!

THOMAS CAMPBELL

## The Good-Morrow

I wonder by my troth, what thou and I
Did, till we loved? Were we not wean'd till then?
But suck'd on country pleasures, childishly?
Or snorted we in the Seven Sleepers' den?
'Twas so; but this, all pleasures fancies be;
If ever any beauty I did see,
Which I desired, and got, 'twas but a dream of thee.

And now good-morrow to our waking souls,
Which watch not one another out of fear;
For love all love of other sights controls,
And makes one little room an everywhere.
Let sea-discoverers to new worlds have gone;
Let maps to other, worlds on worlds have shown;
Let us possess one world; each hath one, and is one.

My face in thine eye, thine in mine appears,
And true plain hearts do in the faces rest;
Where can we find two better hemispheres
Without sharp north, without declining west?
Whatever dies, was not mix'd equally;
If our two loves be one, or thou and I
Love so alike that none can slacken, none can die.

JOHN DONNE

## Over the Roofs

### I

Oh chimes set high on the sunny tower
   Ring on, ring on unendingly,
Make all the hours a single hour,
For when the dusk begins to flower,
   The man I love will come to me! ...

But no, go slowly as you will,
   I should not bid you hasten so,
For while I wait for love to come,
Some other girl is standing dumb,
   Fearing her love will go.

### II

Oh white steam over the roofs, blow high!
   Oh chimes in the tower ring clear and free!
Oh sun awake in the covered sky,
   For the man I love, loves me! ...

Oh drifting steam disperse and die,
   Oh tower stand shrouded toward the south,—
Fate heard afar my happy cry,
   And laid her finger on my mouth.

## III

The dusk was blue with blowing mist,
    The lights were spangles in a veil,
And from the clamor far below
    Floated faint music like a wail.

It voiced what I shall never speak,
    My heart was breaking all night long,
But when the dawn was hard and gray,
    My tears distilled into a song.

## IV

I said, "I have shut my heart
    As one shuts an open door,
That Love may starve therein
    And trouble me no more."

But over the roofs there came
    The wet new wind of May,
And a tune blew up from the curb
    Where the street-pianos play.

My room was white with the sun
    And Love cried out to me,
"I am strong, I will break your heart
    Unless you set me free."

SARA TEASDALE

# Love

All thoughts, all passions, all delights,
Whatever stirs this mortal frame,
All are but ministers of Love,
    And feed his sacred flame.

Oft in my waking dreams do I
Live o'er again that happy hour,
When midway on the mount I lay,
    Beside the ruin'd tower.

The moonshine, stealing o'er the scene,
Had blended with the lights of eve;
And she was there, my hope, my joy,
    My own dear Genevieve!

She lean'd against the armèd man,
The statue of the armèd Knight;
She stood and listen'd to my lay,
    Amid the lingering light.

Few sorrows hath she of her own,
My hope! my joy! my Genevieve!
She loves me best whene'er I sing
    The songs that make her grieve.

I play'd a soft and doleful air;
I sang an old and moving story—
An old rude song, that suited well
    That ruin wild and hoary.

She listen'd with a flitting blush,
With downcast eyes and modest grace;
For well she knew I could not choose
    But gaze upon her face.

I told her of the Knight that wore
Upon his shield a burning brand;
And that for ten long years he woo'd
    The Lady of the Land.

I told her how he pined: and ah!
The deep, the low, the pleading tone
With which I sang another's love,
    Interpreted my own.

She listen'd with a flitting blush,
With downcast eyes, and modest grace;
And she forgave me, that I gazed
    Too fondly on her face!

But when I told the cruel scorn
That crazed that bold and lovely Knight,
And that he cross'd the mountain-woods,
    Nor rested day nor night;

That sometimes from the savage den,
And sometimes from the darksome shade,
And sometimes starting up at once
   In green and sunny glade—

There came and look'd him in the face
An angel beautiful and bright;
And that he knew it was a Fiend,
   This miserable Knight!

And that, unknowing what he did,
He leap'd amid a murderous band,
And saved from outrage worse than death
   The Lady of the Land;—

And how she wept and clasp'd his knees;
And how she tended him in vain—
And ever strove to expiate
   The scorn that crazed his brain;—

And that she nursed him in a cave;
And how his madness went away,
When on the yellow forest leaves
   A dying man he lay;—

His dying words—but when I reach'd
That tenderest strain of all the ditty,
My faltering voice and pausing harp
   Disturb'd her soul with pity!

All impulses of soul and sense
Had thrill'd my guileless Genevieve;
The music and the doleful tale,
    The rich and balmy eve;

And hopes, and fears that kindle hope,
An undistinguishable throng,
And gentle wishes long subdued,
    Subdued and cherish'd long!

She wept with pity and delight,
She blush'd with love and virgin shame;
And like the murmur of a dream,
    I heard her breathe my name.

Her bosom heaved—she stepp'd aside,
As conscious of my look she stept—
Then suddenly, with timorous eye
    She fled to me and wept.

She half enclosed me with her arms,
She press'd me with a meek embrace;
And bending back her head, look'd up,
    And gazed upon my face.

Twas partly love, and partly fear,
And partly 'twas a bashful art,
That I might rather feel, than see,
    The swelling of her heart.

I calm'd her fears, and she was calm,
And told her love with virgin pride;
And so I won my Genevieve,
 My bright and beauteous Bride.

SAMUEL TAYLOR COLERIDGE

## Song

My love is in a light attire
　　Among the apple trees,
Where the gay winds do most desire
　　To run in companies.

There, where the gay winds stay to woo
　　The young leaves as they pass,
My love goes slowly, bending to
　　Her shadow on the grass.

And where the sky's a pale blue cup
　　Over the laughing land,
My love goes lightly, holding up
　　Her dress with dainty hand.

JAMES JOYCE

## How Do I Love Thee?

How do I love thee? Let me count the ways.
I love thee to the depth and breadth and height
My soul can reach, when feeling out of sight
For the ends of being and ideal grace.
I love thee to the level of every day's
Most quiet need, by sun and candle-light.
I love thee freely, as men strive for right.
I love thee purely, as they turn from praise.
I love thee with the passion put to use
In my old griefs, and with my childhood's faith.
I love thee with a love I seemed to lose
With my lost saints. I love thee with the breath,
Smiles, tears, of all my life; and, if God choose,
I shall but love thee better after death.

ELIZABETH BARRETT BROWNING

## Whoever You Are Holding Me Now in Hand

Whoever you are holding me now in hand,
Without one thing all will be useless,
I give you fair warning before you attempt me further,
I am not what you supposed, but far different.

Who is he that would become my follower?
Who would sign himself a candidate for my affections?

The way is suspicious, the result uncertain, perhaps
     destructive,
You would have to give up all else, I alone would expect
     to be your sole and exclusive standard,
Your novitiate would even then be long and exhausting,
The whole past theory of your life and all conformity to
     the lives around you would have to be abandon'd,
Therefore release me now before troubling yourself any
     further, let go your hand from my shoulders,
Put me down and depart on your way.

Or else by stealth in some wood for trial,
Or back of a rock in the open air,
(For in any roof'd room of a house I emerge not, nor in
     company,
And in libraries I lie as one dumb, a gawk, or unborn, or
     dead,)
But just possibly with you on a high hill, first watching
     lest any person for miles around approach unawares,

Or possibly with you sailing at sea, or on the beach of
    the sea or some quiet island,
Here to put your lips upon mine I permit you,
With the comrade's long-dwelling kiss or the new
    husband's kiss,
For I am the new husband and I am the comrade.

Or if you will, thrusting me beneath your clothing,
Where I may feel the throbs of your heart or rest upon
    your hip,
Carry me when you go forth over land or sea;
For thus merely touching you is enough, is best,
And thus touching you would I silently sleep and be
    carried eternally.

But these leaves conning you con at peril,
For these leaves and me you will not understand,
They will elude you at first and still more afterward, I
    will certainly elude you,
Even while you should think you had unquestionably
    caught me, behold!
Already you see I have escaped from you.

For it is not for what I have put into it that I have
    written this book,
Nor is it by reading it you will acquire it,
Nor do those know me best who admire me and
    vauntingly praise me,
Nor will the candidates for my love (unless at most a
    very few) prove victorious,

Nor will my poems do good only, they will do just as
     much evil, perhaps more,
For all is useless without that which you may guess at
     many times and not hit, that which I hinted at;
Therefore release me and depart on your way.

WALT WHITMAN

# I Love You

I love your lips when they're wet with wine
And red with a wild desire;
I love your eyes when the lovelight lies
Lit with a passionate fire.
I love your arms when the warm white flesh
Touches mine in a fond embrace;
I love your hair when the strands enmesh
Your kisses against my face.

Not for me the cold, calm kiss
Of a virgin's bloodless love;
Not for me the saint's white bliss,
Nor the heart of a spotless dove.
But give me the love that so freely gives
And laughs at the whole world's blame,
With your body so young and warm in my arms,
It sets my poor heart aflame.

So kiss me sweet with your warm wet mouth,
Still fragrant with ruby wine,
And say with a fervor born of the South
That your body and soul are mine.
Clasp me close in your warm young arms,
While the pale stars shine above,
And we'll live our whole young lives away
In the joys of a living love.

ELLA WHEELER WILCOX

## Midwinter

All night I dreamed of roses,
  Wild tangle by the sea,
And shadowy garden closes.
  Dream-led I met with thee.

Around thee swayed the roses,
  Beyond thee sang the sea;
The shadowy garden closes
  Were Paradise to me.

O Love, 'mid the dream-roses
  Abide to heal, to save!
The world that day discloses
  Narrows to one white grave.

SOPHIE JEWETT

## Love's Philosophy

The fountains mingle with the river
And the rivers with the ocean,
The winds of heaven mix for ever
With a sweet emotion;
Nothing in the world is single,
All things by a law divine
In one another's being mingle—
Why not I with thine?

See the mountains kiss high heaven,
And the waves clasp one another;
No sister-flower would be forgiven
If it disdain'd its brother;
And the sunlight clasps the earth,
And the moonbeams kiss the sea—
What is all this sweet work worth
If thou kiss not me?

PERCY BYSSHE SHELLEY

## Let Me Not to the Marriage of True Minds

Let me not to the marriage of true minds
Admit impediments. Love is not love
Which alters when it alteration finds,
Or bends with the remover to remove:
O, no! it is an ever-fixed mark,
That looks on tempests and is never shaken;
It is the star to every wandering bark,
Whose worth's unknown, although his height be taken.
Love's not Time's fool, though rosy lips and cheeks
Within his bending sickle's compass come;
Love alters not with his brief hours and weeks,
But bears it out even to the edge of doom.
   If this be error, and upon me prov'd,
   I never writ, nor no man ever lov'd.

WILLIAM SHAKESPEARE

## To My Dear and Loving Husband

If ever two were one, then surely we.
If ever man were loved by wife, then thee;
If ever wife was happy in a man,
Compare with me ye women if you can.
I prize thy love more than whole mines of gold,
Or all the riches that the East doth hold.
My love is such that rivers cannot quench,
Nor ought but love from thee give recompense.
Thy love is such I can no way repay;
The heavens reward thee manifold, I pray.
Then while we live, in love let's so persever,
That when we live no more we may live ever.

ANNE BRADSTREET

## All for Love

O talk not to me of a name great in story;
The days of our youth are the days of our glory;
And the myrtle and ivy of sweet two-and-twenty
Are worth all your laurels, though ever so plenty.

What are garlands and crowns to the brow that is
    wrinkled?
'Tis but as a dead flower with May-dew besprinkled:
Then away with all such from the head that is hoary—
What care I for the wreaths that can only give glory?

O Fame! if I e'er took delight in thy praises,
'Twas less for the sake of thy high-sounding phrases,
Than to see the bright eyes of the dear one discover
She thought that I was not unworthy to love her.

There chiefly I sought thee, there only I found thee;
Her glance was the best of the rays that surround thee;
When it sparkled o'er aught that was bright in my story,
I knew it was love, and I felt it was glory.

LORD BYRON

## When You Are Old

When you are old and grey and full of sleep,
And nodding by the fire, take down this book,
And slowly read, and dream of the soft look
Your eyes had once, and of their shadows deep;

How many loved your moments of glad grace,
And loved your beauty with love false or true,
But one man loved the pilgrim soul in you,
And loved the sorrows of your changing face;

And bending down beside the glowing bars,
Murmur, a little sadly, how Love fled
And paced upon the mountains overhead
And hid his face amid a crowd of stars.

WILLIAM BUTLER YEATS

## Debt

What do I owe to you
Who loved me deep and long?
You never gave my spirit wings
Nor gave my heart a song.

But oh, to him I loved,
Who loved me not at all,
I owe the little open gate
That led through heaven's wall.

SARA TEASDALE

## Faults

They came to tell your faults to me,
They named them over one by one;
I laughed aloud when they were done,
I knew them all so well before, —
Oh, they were blind, too blind to see
Your faults had made me love you more.

SARA TEASDALE

# The Flight of Love

When the lamp is shatter'd,
The light in the dust lies dead—
When the cloud is scatter'd,
The rainbow's glory is shed.
When the lute is broken,
Sweet tones are remember'd not;
When the lips have spoken,
Loved accents are soon forgot.

As music and splendour
Survive not the lamp and the lute,
The heart's echoes render
No song when the spirit is mute—
No song but sad dirges,
Like the wind through a ruin'd cell,
Or the mournful surges
That ring the dead seaman's knell.

When hearts have once mingled,
Love first leaves the well-built nest;
The weak one is singled
To endure what it once possest.
O Love! who bewailest
The frailty of all things here,
Why choose you the frailest
For your cradle, your home, and your bier?

Its passions will rock thee
As the storms rock the ravens on high;
Bright reason will mock thee
Like the sun from a wintry sky.
From thy nest every rafter
Will rot, and thine eagle home
Leave thee naked to laughter,
When leaves fall and cold winds come.

PERCY BYSSHE SHELLEY

## At a Window

Give me hunger,
O you gods that sit and give
The world its orders.
Give me hunger, pain and want,
Shut me out with shame and failure
From your doors of gold and fame,
Give me your shabbiest, weariest hunger!

But leave me a little love,
A voice to speak to me in the day end,
A hand to touch me in the dark room
Breaking the long loneliness.
In the dusk of day-shapes
Blurring the sunset,
One little wandering, western star
Thrust out from the changing shores of shadow.
Let me go to the window,
Watch there the day-shapes of dusk
And wait and know the coming
Of a little love.

CARL SANDBURG

## I Am Not Yours

I am not yours, not lost in you,
Not lost, although I long to be
Lost as a candle lit at noon,
Lost as a snowflake in the sea.

You love me, and I find you still
A spirit beautiful and bright,
Yet I am I, who long to be
Lost as a light is lost in light.

Oh plunge me deep in love—put out
My senses, leave me deaf and blind,
Swept by the tempest of your love,
A taper in a rushing wind.

SARA TEASDALE

## Defeated

When the last fight is lost, the last sword broken;
The last call sounded, the last order spoken;
When from the field where braver hearts lie sleeping,
Faint, and athirst, and blinded, I come creeping,
With not one waving shred of palm to bring you,
With not one splendid battle-song to sing you,
O Love, in my dishonor and defeat,
Your measureless compassion will be sweet.

SOPHIE JEWETT

## When We Two Parted

When we two parted
In silence and tears,
Half broken-hearted
To sever for years,
Pale grew thy cheek and cold,
Colder thy kiss;
Truly that hour foretold
Sorrow to this!

The dew of the morning
Sunk chill on my brow;
It felt like the warning
Of what I feel now.
Thy vows are all broken,
And light is thy fame:
I hear thy name spoken,
And share in its shame.

They name thee before me,
A knell to mine ear;
A shudder comes o'er me—
Why wert thou so dear?
They know not I knew thee,
Who knew thee too well:
Long, long shall I rue thee
Too deeply to tell.

In secret we met:
In silence I grieve
That thy heart could forget,
Thy spirit deceive.
If I should meet thee
After long years,
How should I greet thee?—
With silence and tears.

LORD BYRON

## If I Had Known

If I had known
Two years ago how drear this life should be,
And crowd upon itself allstrangely sad,
Mayhap another song would burst from out my lips,
Overflowing with the happiness of future hopes;
Mayhap another throb than that of joy.
Have stirred my soul into its inmost depths,
       If I had known.

If I had known,
Two years ago the impotence of love,
The vainness of a kiss, how barren a caress,
Mayhap my soul to higher things have soarn,
Nor clung to earthly loves and tender dreams,
But ever up aloft into the blue empyrean,
And there to master all the world of mind,
       If I had known.

ALICE MOORE DUNBAR-NELSON

## Remember

Remember me when I am gone away,
  Gone far away into the silent land;
  When you can no more hold me by the hand,
Nor I half turn to go yet turning stay.
Remember me when no more day by day
  You tell me of our future that you planned:
  Only remember me; you understand
It will be late to counsel then or pray.
Yet if you should forget me for a while
  And afterwards remember, do not grieve:
  For if the darkness and corruption leave
  A vestige of the thoughts that once I had,
Better by far you should forget and smile
  Than that you should remember and be sad.

CHRISTINA ROSSETTI

## Forget not Yet

Forget not yet the tried intent
Of such a truth as I have meant;
My great travail so gladly spent,
    Forget not yet.

  Forget not yet when first began
The weary life ye know, since whan
The suit, the service, none tell can;
    Forget not yet.

  Forget not yet the great assays,
The cruel wrong, the scornful ways;
The painful patience in denays,
    Forget not yet.

  Forget not yet, forget not this,
How long ago hath been and is
The mind that never meant amiss;
    Forget not yet.

  Forget not then thine own approved,
The which so long hath thee so loved,
Whose steadfast faith yet never moved;
    Forget not this.

SIR THOMAS WYATT

## Never Give all the Heart

Never give all the heart, for love
Will hardly seem worth thinking of
To passionate women if it seem
Certain, and they never dream
That it fades out from kiss to kiss;
For everything that's lovely is
But a brief, dreamy, kind delight.
O never give the heart outright,
For they, for all smooth lips can say,
Have given their hearts up to the play.
And who could play it well enough
If deaf and dumb and blind with love?
He that made this knows all the cost,
For he gave all his heart and lost.

WILLIAM BUTLER YEATS

## Time and Love

When I have seen by Time's fell hand defaced
The rich proud cost of out-worn buried age;
When sometime lofty towers I see down-razed,
And brass eternal slave to mortal rage.

When I have seen the hungry ocean gain
Advantage on the kingdom of the shore,
And the firm soil win of the watery main,
Increasing store with loss, and loss with store.

When I have seen such interchange of state,
Or state itself confounded to decay,
Ruin hath taught me thus to ruminate—
That Time will come and take my Love away.

—This thought is as a death, which cannot choose
But weep to have that which it fears to lose.

WILLIAM SHAKESPEARE

## A Reminiscence

Yes, thou art gone and never more
Thy sunny smile shall gladden me;
But I may pass the old church door
And pace the floor that covers thee;

May stand upon the cold, damp stone,
And think that frozen lies below
The lightest heart that I have known,
The kindest I shall ever know.

Yet, though I cannot see thee more
Tis still a comfort to have seen,
And though thy transient life is o'er
Tis sweet to think that thou hast been;

To think a soul so near divine,
Within a form so angel fair
United to a heart like thine
Has gladdened once our humble sphere.

ANNE BRONTË

## One Day I Wrote her Name

One day I wrote her name upon the strand,
But came the waves and washed it away:
Again I wrote it with a second hand,
But came the tide, and made my pains his prey.
"Vain man," said she, "that dost in vain assay,
A mortal thing so to immortalize;
For I myself shall like to this decay,
And eke my name be wiped out likewise."
"Not so," (quod I) "let baser things devise
To die in dust, but you shall live by fame:
My verse your vertues rare shall eternize,
And in the heavens write your glorious name:
Where whenas death shall all the world subdue,
Our love shall live, and later life renew."

EDMUND SPENSER

# The Last Rose of Summer

'Tis the last rose of Summer,
  Left blooming alone;
All her lovely companions
  Are faded and gone;
No flower of her kindred,
  No rose-bud is nigh,
To reflect back her blushes
  Or give sigh for sigh!

I'll not leave thee, thou lone one,
  To pine on the stem;
Since the lovely are sleeping,
  Go sleep thou with them.
Thus kindly I scatter
  Thy leaves o'er the bed
Where thy mates of the garden
  Lie scentless and dead.

So soon may I follow,
  When friendships decay,
And from Love's shining circle
  The gems drop away!
When true hearts lie withered,
  And fond ones are flown,
Oh! who would inhabit
  This bleak world alone?

THOMAS MOORE

# Reunited

Let us begin, dear love, where we left off;
　Tie up the broken threads of that old dream;
　And go on happy as before; and seem
Lovers again, though all the world may scoff.

Let us forget the graves, which lie between
　Our parting and our meeting, and the tears
　That rusted out the goldwork of the years;
The frosts that fell upon our gardens green.

Let us forget the cold malicious fate
　Who made our loving hearts her idle toys,
　And once more revel in the old sweet joys
Of happy love. Nay, it is not too late!

Forget the deep-ploughed furrows in my brow;
　Forget the silver gleaming in my hair;
　Look only in my eyes! Oh! darling, there
The old love shone no warmer then than now.

Down in the tender depths of thy dear eyes,
　I find the lost sweet memory of my youth,
　Bright with the holy radiance of thy truth,
And hallowed with the blue of summer skies.

Tie up the broken threads, and let us go,
　Like reunited lovers, hand in hand,
　Back, and yet onward, to the sunny land,
Of our To Be, which was our Long Ago.

ELLA WHEELER WILCOX

# Part V

~

# Spirituality

# Invocation

Rarely, rarely, comest thou,
  Spirit of Delight!
Wherefore hast thou left me now
  Many a day and night?
Many a weary night and day
Tis since thou art fled away.

How shall ever one like me
  Win thee back again?
With the joyous and the free
  Thou wilt scoff at pain.
Spirit false! thou hast forgot
All but those who need thee not.

As a lizard with the shade
  Of a trembling leaf,
Thou with sorrow art dismay'd;
  Even the sighs of grief
Reproach thee, that thou art not near,
And reproach thou wilt not hear.

Let me set my mournful ditty
  To a merry measure;—
Thou wilt never come for pity,
  Thou wilt come for pleasure;—
Pity then will cut away
Those cruel wings, and thou wilt stay.

I love all that thou lovest,
　　Spirit of Delight!
The fresh Earth in new leaves drest
　　And the starry night;
Autumn evening, and the morn
When the golden mists are born.

I love snow, and all the forms
　　Of the radiant frost;
I love waves, and winds, and storms,
　　Everything almost
Which is Nature's, and may be
Untainted by man's misery.

I love tranquil solitude,
　　And such society
As is quiet, wise, and good;
　　Between thee and me
What diff'rence? but thou dost possess
The things I seek, not love them less.

I love Love—though he has wings,
　　And like light can flee,
But above all other things,
　　Spirit, I love thee—
Thou art love and life! O come!
Make once more my heart thy home!

PERCY BYSSHE SHELLEY

# All the World's a Stage

All the world's a stage,
And all the men and women merely players;
They have their exits and their entrances;
And one man in his time plays many parts,
His acts being seven ages. At first the infant,
Mewling and puking in the nurse's arms;
And then the whining school-boy, with his satchel
And shining morning face, creeping like snail
Unwillingly to school. And then the lover,
Sighing like furnace, with a woeful ballad
Made to his mistress' eyebrow. Then a soldier,
Full of strange oaths, and bearded like the pard,
Jealous in honour, sudden and quick in quarrel,
Seeking the bubble reputation
Even in the cannon's mouth. And then the justice,
In fair round belly with good capon lin'd,
With eyes severe and beard of formal cut,
Full of wise saws and modern instances;
And so he plays his part. The sixth age shifts
Into the lean and slipper'd pantaloon,
With spectacles on nose and pouch on side;
His youthful hose, well sav'd, a world too wide
For his shrunk shank; and his big manly voice,
Turning again toward childish treble, pipes
And whistles in his sound. Last scene of all,
That ends this strange eventful history,
Is second childishness and mere oblivion;
Sans teeth, sans eyes, sans taste, sans everything.

                                    WILLIAM SHAKESPEARE

# Eden

A learned and a happy ignorance
    Divided me
  From all the vanity,
From all the sloth, care, pain, and sorrow that advance
    The madness and the misery
Of men. No error, no distraction I
Saw soil the earth, or overcloud the sky.

  I knew not that there was a serpent's sting,
    Whose poison shed
    On men, did overspread
The world; nor did I dream of such a thing
    As sin, in which mankind lay dead.
They all were brisk and living wights to me,
Yea, pure and full of immortality.

  Joy, pleasure, beauty, kindness, glory, love,
    Sleep, day, life, light,
    Peace, melody, my sight,
My ears and heart did fill and freely move.
    All that I saw did me delight.
The Universe was then a world of treasure,
To me an universal world of pleasure.

  Unwelcome penitence was then unknown,
    Vain costly toys,
    Swearing and roaring boys,
Shops, markets, taverns, coaches, were unshown;

So all things were that drown'd my joys:
No thorns chok'd up my path, nor hid the face
Of bliss and beauty, nor eclips'd the place.

Only what Adam in his first estate,
    Did I behold;
  Hard silver and dry gold
As yet lay under ground; my blessed fate
   Was more acquainted with the old
And innocent delights which he did see
In his original simplicity.

Those things which first his Eden did adorn,
    My infancy
  Did crown. Simplicity
Was my protection when I first was born.
   Mine eyes those treasures first did see
Which God first made. The first effects of love
My first enjoyments upon earth did prove;

And were so great, and so divine, so pure;
    So fair and sweet,
  So true; when I did meet
Them here at first, they did my soul allure,
   And drew away my infant feet
Quite from the works of men; that I might see
The glorious wonders of the Deity.

THOMAS TRAHERNE

## The Incarnate

Deep in the soul there throbs the secret pain
Of one homesick for dear familiar things,
When Spring winds rock the waves of sunlit rain
And on the grass there falls the shadow of wings.

How should one bend one's dreams to the dark clay
Where carven beauty mixed with madness dwells?
And men who fear to die fear not to slay,
And Life has built herself ten thousand hells.

No wave that breaks in music on the shore
Can purify the tiger's bloodstained den,
The worms that crawl about the dark world's core
Cry out aloud against the deeds of men.

Alas, the peace of these still hours and deep
Is but a dream that wanders from afar,
And the great Dreamer, turning in His sleep,
Smothers in darkness all our little star.

Yet in the gentle spirit of the wise
Light flashes out through many a simple thing,
The tired ploughman, with impassive eyes,
Knows in his heart that he was once a king.

He sees in dreams the crown long lost and dear,
That glittered on a fallen spirit's brow,
A shattered gleam from some far shining sphere
Has dazed the eyes of him who drives the plough.

The long brown furrows of the broken soil
Lead in straight lines unto the sunset's gates;
On high green hills, beyond the reach of toil,
The vision of the twilight broods and waits.

The silence folded in about the heart
Whispers strange longings to the broken soul,
That lingers in a lonely place apart,
Stretching vain hands to clasp the secret whole.

EVA GORE-BOOTH

## Of Mans First Disobedience

Of Mans First Disobedience, and the Fruit
Of that Forbidden Tree, whose mortal tast
Brought Death into the World, and all our woe,
With loss of Eden, till one greater Man
Restore us, and regain the blissful Seat,
Sing Heav'nly Muse, that on the secret top
Of Oreb, or of Sinai, didst inspire
That Shepherd, who first taught the chosen Seed,
In the Beginning how the Heav'ns and Earth
Rose out of Chaos: or if Sion Hill
Delight thee more, and Siloa's brook that flow'd
Fast by the Oracle of God; I thence
Invoke thy aid to my adventrous Song,
That with no middle flight intends to soar
Above th' Aonian Mount, while it pursues
Things unattempted yet in Prose or Rhime.
And chiefly Thou, O Spirit, that dost prefer
Before all Temples th' upright heart and pure,
Instruct me, for Thou know'st; Thou from the first
Wast present, and with mighty wings outspread
Dove-like satst brooding on the vast Abyss
And mad'st it pregnant: What in me is dark
Illumin, what is low raise and support;
That to the highth of this great Argument
I may assert Eternal Providence,
And justifie the wayes of God to men.

Say first, for Heav'n hides nothing from thy view
Nor the deep Tract of Hell, say first what cause
Mov'd our Grand Parents in that happy State,
Favour'd of Heav'n so highly, to fall off
From thir Creator, and transgress his Will
For one restraint, Lords of the World besides?
Who first seduc'd them to that foul revolt?
Th' infernal Serpent; he it was, whose guile
Stird up with Envy and Revenge, deceiv'd
The Mother of Mankind, what time his Pride
Had cast him out from Heav'n, with all his Host
Of Rebel Angels, by whose aid aspiring
To set himself in Glory above his Peers,
He trusted to have equal'd the most High,
If he oppos'd; and with ambitious aim
Against the Throne and Monarchy of God
Rais'd impious War in Heav'n and Battel proud
With vain attempt.   Him the Almighty Power
Hurld headlong flaming from th' Ethereal Skie
With hideous ruine and combustion down
To bottomless perdition, there to dwell
In Adamantine Chains and penal Fire,
Who durst defie th' Omnipotent to Arms.
Nine times the Space that measures Day and Night
To mortal men, he with his horrid crew
Lay vanquisht, rowling in the fiery Gulfe
Confounded though immortal: But his doom
Reserv'd him to more wrath; for now the thought
Both of lost happiness and lasting pain
Torments him; round he throws his baleful eyes

That witness'd huge affliction and dismay
Mixt with obdurate pride and stedfast hate:
At once as far as Angels kenn he views
The dismal Situation waste and wilde,
A Dungeon horrible, on all sides round
As one great Furnace flam'd, yet from those flames
No light, but rather darkness visible
Serv'd onely to discover sights of woe,
Regions of sorrow, doleful shades, where peace
And rest can never dwell, hope never comes
That comes to all; but torture without end
Still urges, and a fiery Deluge, fed
With ever-burning Sulphur unconsum'd:
Such place Eternal Justice had prepar'd
For those rebellious, here thir prison ordained
In utter darkness, and thir portion set
As far remov'd from God and light of Heav'n
As from the Center thrice to th' utmost Pole.
O how unlike the place from whence they fell!
There the companions of his fall, o'rewhelm'd
With Floods and Whirlwinds of tempestuous fire,
He soon discerns, and weltring by his side
One next himself in power, and next in crime,
Long after known in Palestine, and nam'd
Beelzebub.   To whom th' Arch-Enemy,
And thence in Heav'n call'd Satan, with bold words
Breaking the horrid silence thus began.

JOHN MILTON

## A Daughter of Eve

A fool I was to sleep at noon,
And wake when night is chilly
Beneath the comfortless cold moon;
A fool to pluck my rose too soon,
A fool to snap my lily.

My garden-plot I have not kept;
Faded and all-forsaken,
I weep as I have never wept:
Oh it was summer when I slept,
It's winter now I waken.

Talk what you please of future spring
And sun-warm'd sweet to-morrow:—
Stripp'd bare of hope and everything,
No more to laugh, no more to sing,
I sit alone with sorrow.

CHRISTINA ROSSETTI

## The Inner Vision

Most sweet it is with unuplifted eyes
To pace the ground, if path there be or none,
While a fair region round the Traveller lies
Which he forbears again to look upon;

Pleased rather with some soft ideal scene
The work of Fancy, or some happy tone
Of meditation, slipping in between
The beauty coming and the beauty gone.

—If Thought and Love desert us, from that day
Let us break off all commerce with the Muse:
With Thought and Love companions of our way—

Whate'er the senses take or may refuse,—
The Mind's internal heaven shall shed her dews
Of inspiration on the humblest lay.

WILLIAM WORDSWORTH

# The Body to the Soul

You have dragged me on through the wild wood ways,
You have given me toil and scanty rest,
I have seen the light of ten thousand days
Grow dim and sink and fade in the West.

Once you bore me forth from the dusty gloom,
Weeping and helpless and naked and blind,
Now you would hide me deep down in the tomb,
And wander away on the moonlit wind.

You would bury me like a thing of shame,
Silently into the darkness thrust,
You would mix my heart that was once a flame
With the mouldering clay and the wandering dust.

The eyes that wept for your sorrowful will
Shall be laid among evil and unclean things,
The heart that was faithful through good and ill
You scorn for a flutter of tawdry wings.

You were the moonlight, I lived in the sun;
Could there ever be peace between us twain?
I sought the Many, you seek the One,
You are the slayer, I am the slain.

Oh soul, when you mount to your flame-built throne
Will you dream no dream of the broken clay?
Will you breathe o'er the stars in your pathway strown,
No sigh for the daisies of yesterday?

As you wander the shining corridors,
A lonely wave in the ocean of light,
Have you never a thought of the lake's lost shores,
Or the fire-lit cottage dim and white?

Shall not the dear smell of the rain-wet soil
Through the windless spheres and the silence float?
Shall not my hands that are brown with toil
Take your dreams and high desires by the throat?

Behold, I reach forth from beyond the years,
I will cry to you from beneath the sod,
I will drag you back from the starry spheres,
Yea, down from the very bosom of God.

You cannot hide from the sun and the wind,
Or the whispered song of the April rain,
The proud earth that moulds all things to her mind,
Shall gather you out of the deeps again.

You shall follow once more a wandering fire,
You shall gaze again on the starlit sea,
You shall gather roses out of the mire:
Alas, but you shall not remember me.

EVA GORE-BOOTH

# Morality

We cannot kindle when we will
The fire which in the heart resides;
The spirit bloweth and is still,
In mystery our soul abides.
But tasks in hours of insight will'd
Can be through hours of gloom fulfill'd.

With aching hands and bleeding feet
We dig and heap, lay stone on stone;
We bear the burden and the heat
Of the long day, and wish 'twere done.
Not till the hours of light return,
All we have built do we discern.

Then, when the clouds are off the soul,
When thou dost bask in Nature's eye,
Ask, how she view'd thy self-control,
Thy struggling, task'd morality—
Nature, whose free, light, cheerful air,
Oft made thee, in thy gloom, despair.

And she, whose censure thou dost dread,
Whose eye thou wast afraid to seek,
See, on her face a glow is spread,
A strong emotion on her cheek!
Ah, child! she cries, "that strife divine,
Whence was it, for it is not mine?

There is no effort on my brow—
I do not strive, I do not weep;
I rush with the swift spheres and glow
In joy, and when I will, I sleep.
Yet that severe, that earnest air,
I saw, I felt it once—but where?

I knew not yet the gauge of time,"
Nor wore the manacles of space;
I felt it in some other clime,
I saw it in some other place.
Twas when the heavenly house I trod,
And lay upon the breast of God."

MATTHEW ARNOLD

The Unspeakable

*by Alisha B.*

I come from the land of spirits
I come from behind you
You think it's your future
It is a deeper past
than you will remember in this lifetime
It is dark because it's behind you
It is as cool as the shadows' pockets

You come from the dark into the light
You walk facing the sun
You do not want to remember
You cannot remember
although you sit all night, mouth open
I am always behind you
a hand a breath
nothing that reminds you entirely
of your death

SILVERWATER POETS

# No Coward Soul Is Mine

No coward soul is mine
No trembler in the world's storm-troubled sphere
I see Heaven's glories shine
And Faith shines equal arming me from Fear

O God within my breast
Almighty ever-present Deity
Life, that in me hast rest,
As I Undying Life, have power in Thee

Vain are the thousand creeds
That move men's hearts, unutterably vain,
Worthless as withered weeds
Or idlest froth amid the boundless main

To waken doubt in one
Holding so fast by thy infinity,
So surely anchored on
The steadfast rock of Immortality.

With wide-embracing love
Thy spirit animates eternal years
Pervades and broods above,
Changes, sustains, dissolves, creates and rears

Though earth and moon were gone
And suns and universes ceased to be
And Thou wert left alone
Every Existence would exist in thee

There is not room for Death
Nor atom that his might could render void
Since thou art Being and Breath
And what thou art may never be destroyed.

EMILY BRONTË

## The Living Temple

Not in the world of light alone,
Where God has built his blazing throne,
Nor yet alone in earth below,
With belted seas that come and go,
And endless isles of sunlit green,
Is all thy Maker's glory seen:
Look in upon thy wondrous frame,—
Eternal wisdom still the same!

The smooth, soft air with pulse-like waves
Flows murmuring through its hidden caves,
Whose streams of brightening purple rush,
Fired with a new and livelier blush,
While all their burden of decay
The ebbing current steals away,
And red with Nature's flame they start
From the warm fountains of the heart.

No rest that throbbing slave may ask,
Forever quivering o'er his task,
While far and wide a crimson jet
Leaps forth to fill the woven net
Which in unnumbered crossing tides
The flood of burning life divides,
Then, kindling each decaying part,
Creeps back to find the throbbing heart.

But warmed with that unchanging flame
Behold the outward moving frame,
Its living marbles jointed strong
With glistening band and silvery thong,
And linked to reason's guiding reins
By myriad rings in trembling chains,
Each graven with the threaded zone
Which claims it as the master's own.

See how yon beam of seeming white
Is braided out of seven-hued light,
Yet in those lucid globes no ray
By any chance shall break astray.
Hark how the rolling surge of sound,
Arches and spirals circling round,
Wakes the hushed spirit through thine ear
With music it is heaven to hear.

Then mark the cloven sphere that holds
All thought in its mysterious folds;
That feels sensation's faintest thrill,
And flashes forth the sovereign will;
Think on the stormy world that dwells
Locked in its dim and clustering cells!
The lightning gleams of power it sheds
Along its hollow glassy threads!

O Father! grant thy love divine
To make these mystic temples thine!

When wasting age and wearying strife
Have sapped the leaning walls of life,
When darkness gathers over all,
And the last tottering pillars fall,
Take the poor dust thy mercy warms,
And mould it into heavenly forms!

OLIVER WENDELL HOLMES SR.

## A Dream

In visions of the dark night
I have dreamed of joy departed—
But a waking dream of life and light
Hath left me broken-hearted.

Ah! what is not a dream by day
To him whose eyes are cast
On things around him with a ray
Turned back upon the past?

That holy dream—that holy dream,
While all the world were chiding,
Hath cheered me as a lovely beam
A lonely spirit guiding.

What though that light, thro' storm and night,
So trembled from afar—
What could there be more purely bright
In Truth's day-star?

EDGAR ALLAN POE

# Prometheus

Titan! to whose immortal eyes
    The sufferings of mortality,
    Seen in their sad reality,
Were not as things that gods despise;
What was thy pity's recompense?
A silent suffering, and intense;
The rock, the vulture, and the chain,
All that the proud can feel of pain,
The agony they do not show,
The suffocating sense of woe,
    Which speaks but in its loneliness,
And then is jealous lest the sky
Should have a listener, nor will sigh
    Until its voice is echoless.

Titan! to thee the strife was given
    Between the suffering and the will,
    Which torture where they cannot kill;
And the inexorable Heaven,
And the deaf tyranny of Fate,
The ruling principle of Hate,
Which for its pleasure doth create
The things it may annihilate,
Refus'd thee even the boon to die:
The wretched gift Eternity

Was thine—and thou hast borne it well.
All that the Thunderer wrung from thee
Was but the menace which flung back
On him the torments of thy rack;
The fate thou didst so well foresee,
But would not to appease him tell;
And in thy Silence was his Sentence,
And in his Soul a vain repentance,
And evil dread so ill dissembled,
That in his hand the lightnings trembled.

Thy Godlike crime was to be kind,
      To render with thy precepts less
      The sum of human wretchedness,
And strengthen Man with his own mind;
But baffled as thou wert from high,
Still in thy patient energy,
In the endurance, and repulse
      Of thine impenetrable Spirit,
Which Earth and Heaven could not convulse,
      A mighty lesson we inherit:
Thou art a symbol and a sign
      To Mortals of their fate and force;
Like thee, Man is in part divine,
      A troubled stream from a pure source;
And Man in portions can foresee
His own funereal destiny;
His wretchedness, and his resistance,
And his sad unallied existence:

To which his Spirit may oppose
Itself—and equal to all woes,

And a firm will, and a deep sense,
Which even in torture can descry
    Its own concenter'd recompense,
Triumphant where it dares defy,
And making Death a Victory.

LORD BYRON

## Ode on a Grecian Urn

Thou still unravish'd bride of quietness,
   Thou foster-child of Silence and slow Time,
Sylvan historian, who canst thus express
   A flowery tale more sweetly than our rhyme:
What leaf-fring'd legend haunts about thy shape
   Of deities or mortals, or of both,
     In Tempe or the dales of Arcady?
What men or gods are these? What maidens loth?
   What mad pursuit? What struggle to escape?
     What pipes and timbrels? What wild ecstasy?

Heard melodies are sweet, but those unheard
   Are sweeter; therefore, ye soft pipes, play on;
Not to the sensual ear, but, more endear'd,
   Pipe to the spirit ditties of no tone:
Fair youth, beneath the trees, thou canst not leave
   Thy song, nor ever can those trees be bare;
     Bold lover, never, never canst thou kiss,
Though winning near the goal—yet, do not grieve;
   She cannot fade, though thou hast not thy bliss,
     For ever wilt thou love, and she be fair!

Ah, happy, happy boughs! that cannot shed
   Your leaves, nor ever bid the Spring adieu;
And, happy melodist, unwearied,
   For ever piping songs for ever new;
More happy love! more happy, happy love!
   For ever warm and still to be enjoy'd,

For ever panting, and for ever young;
All breathing human passion far above,
   That leaves a heart high-sorrowful and cloy'd,
      A burning forehead, and a parching tongue.

Who are these coming to the sacrifice?
   To what green altar, O mysterious priest,
Lead'st thou that heifer lowing at the skies,
   And all her silken flanks with garlands drest?
What little town by river or sea shore,
   Or mountain-built with peaceful citadel,
      Is emptied of this folk, this pious morn?
And, little town, thy streets for evermore
   Will silent be; and not a soul to tell
      Why thou art desolate, can e'er return.

O Attic shape! Fair attitude! with brede
   Of marble men and maidens overwrought,
With forest branches and the trodden weed;
   Thou, silent form, dost tease us out of thought
As doth eternity: Cold pastoral!
   When old age shall this generation waste,
      Thou shalt remain, in midst of other woe
Than ours, a friend to man, to whom thou say'st,
   "Beauty is truth, truth beauty"—that is all
      Ye know on earth, and all ye need to know.

JOHN KEATS

# If—

*('Brother Square-Toes'—Rewards and Fairies)*

If you can keep your head when all about you
   Are losing theirs and blaming it on you,
If you can trust yourself when all men doubt you,
   But make allowance for their doubting too;
If you can wait and not be tired by waiting,
   Or being lied about, don't deal in lies,
Or being hated, don't give way to hating,
   And yet don't look too good, nor talk too wise:

If you can dream—and not make dreams your master;
   If you can think—and not make thoughts your aim;
If you can meet with Triumph and Disaster
   And treat those two impostors just the same;
If you can bear to hear the truth you've spoken
   Twisted by knaves to make a trap for fools,
Or watch the things you gave your life to, broken,
   And stoop and build 'em up with worn-out tools:

If you can make one heap of all your winnings
   And risk it on one turn of pitch-and-toss,
And lose, and start again at your beginnings
   And never breathe a word about your loss;
If you can force your heart and nerve and sinew
   To serve your turn long after they are gone,
And so hold on when there is nothing in you
   Except the Will which says to them: 'Hold on!'

If you can talk with crowds and keep your virtue,
    Or walk with Kings—nor lose the common touch,
If neither foes nor loving friends can hurt you,
    If all men count with you, but none too much;
If you can fill the unforgiving minute
    With sixty seconds' worth of distance run,
Yours is the Earth and everything that's in it,
    And—which is more—you'll be a Man, my son!

RUDYARD KIPLING

# The Future

A wanderer is man from his birth.
He was born in a ship
On the breast of the river of Time;
Brimming with wonder and joy
He spreads out his arms to the light,
Rivets his gaze on the banks of the stream.

As what he sees is, so have his thoughts been.
Whether he wakes,
Where the snowy mountainous pass,
Echoing the screams of the eagles,
Hems in its gorges the bed
Of the new-born clear-flowing stream;
Whether he first sees light
Where the river in gleaming rings
Sluggishly winds through the plain;
Whether in sound of the swallowing sea—
As is the world on the banks,
So is the mind of the man.

Vainly does each, as he glides,
Fable and dream
Of the lands which the river of Time
Had left ere he woke on its breast,
Or shall reach when his eyes have been closed.
Only the tract where he sails
He wots of; only the thoughts,
Raised by the objects he passes, are his.

Who can see the green earth any more
As she was by the sources of Time?
Who imagines her fields as they lay
In the sunshine, unworn by the plough?
Who thinks as they thought,
The tribes who then roam'd on her breast,
Her vigorous, primitive sons?

What girl
Now reads in her bosom as clear
As Rebekah read, when she sate
At eve by the palm-shaded well?
Who guards in her breast
As deep, as pellucid a spring
Of feeling, as tranquil, as sure?

What bard,
At the height of his vision, can deem
Of God, of the world, of the soul,
With a plainness as near,
As flashing as Moses felt
When he lay in the night by his flock
On the starlit Arabian waste?
Can rise and obey
The beck of the Spirit like him?

This tract which the river of Time
Now flows through with us, is the plain.
Gone is the calm of its earlier shore.
Border'd by cities and hoarse

With a thousand cries is its stream.
And we on its breast, our minds
Are confused as the cries which we hear,
Changing and shot as the sights which we see.

And we say that repose has fled
For ever the course of the river of Time.
That cities will crowd to its edge
In a blacker, incessanter line;
That the din will be more on its banks,
Denser the trade on its stream,
Flatter the plain where it flows,
Fiercer the sun overhead.
That never will those on its breast
See an ennobling sight,
Drink of the feeling of quiet again.

But what was before us we know not,
And we know not what shall succeed.

Haply, the river of Time—
As it grows, as the towns on its marge
Fling their wavering lights
On a wider, statelier stream—
May acquire, if not the calm
Of its early mountainous shore,
Yet a solemn peace of its own.

And the width of the waters, the hush
Of the grey expanse where he floats,

Freshening its current and spotted with foam
As it draws to the Ocean, may strike
Peace to the soul of the man on its breast—
As the pale waste widens around him,
As the banks fade dimmer away,
As the stars come out, and the night-wind
Brings up the stream
Murmurs and scents of the infinite sea.

MATTHEW ARNOLD

## On His Blindness

When I consider how my light is spent
Ere half my days, in this dark world and wide,
And that one talent which is death to hide
Lodged with me useless, though my soul more bent

To serve therewith my Maker, and present
My true account, lest He returning chide,—
Doth God exact day-labour, light denied?
I fondly ask:—But Patience, to prevent

That murmur, soon replies; God doth not need
Either man's work, or His own gifts: who best
Bear His mild yoke, they serve Him best: His state

Is kingly; thousands at His bidding speed
And post o'er land and ocean without rest:—
They also serve who only stand and wait.

JOHN MILTON

## Character of a Happy Life

How happy is he born and taught
That serveth not another's will;
Whose armour is his honest thought
And simple truth his utmost skill!

Whose passions not his masters are,
Whose soul is still prepared for death,
Not tied unto the world by care
Of public fame, or private breath;

Who envies none that chance doth raise
Or vice; Who never understood
How deepest wounds are given by praise;
Nor rules of state, but rules of good:

Who hath his life from rumours freed,
Whose conscience is his strong retreat;
Whose state can neither flatterers feed,
Nor ruin make accusers great;

Who God doth late and early pray
More of His grace than gifts to lend;
And entertains the harmless day
With a well-chosen book or friend;

—This man is freed from servile bands
Of hope to rise, or fear to fall;
Lord of himself, though not of lands,
And having nothing, yet hath all.

SIR HENRY WOTTON

# A Dream Within a Dream

Take this kiss upon the brow!
And, in parting from you now,
Thus much let me avow —
You are not wrong, who deem
That my days have been a dream;
Yet if hope has flown away
In a night, or in a day,
In a vision, or in none,
Is it therefore the less gone?
All that we see or seem
Is but a dream within a dream.

I stand amid the roar
Of a surf-tormented shore,
And I hold within my hand
Grains of the golden sand —
How few! yet how they creep
Through my fingers to the deep,
While I weep — while I weep!
O God! Can I not grasp
Them with a tighter clasp?
O God! can I not save
One from the pitiless wave?
Is all that we see or seem
But a dream within a dream?

EDGAR ALLAN POE

# At a Solemn Music

Blest pair of Sirens, pledges of Heaven's joy,
Sphere-born harmonious Sisters, Voice, and Verse,
Wed your divine sounds, and mixt power employ
Dead things with inbreathed sense able to pierce,
And to our high-raised phantasy present
That undisturbéd Song of pure concent,
Ay sung before the sapphire-colour'd throne
  To Him that sits thereon,
With saintly shout and solemn jubilee;
Where the bright Seraphim in burning row
Their loud uplifted angel-trumpets blow;
And the Cherubic host in thousand quires
Touch their immortal harps of golden wires,
With those just Spirits that wear victorious palms
  Hymns devout and holy psalms
  Singing everlastingly:
That we on earth, with undiscording voice
May rightly answer that melodious noise;
As once we did, till disproportion'd sin
Jarr'd against nature's chime, and with harsh din
Broke the fair music that all creatures made
To their great Lord, whose love their motion sway'd
In perfect diapason, whilst they stood
In first obedience, and their state of good.
O may we soon again renew that Song,
And keep in tune with Heaven, till God ere long
To His celestial consort us unite,
To live with Him, and sing in endless morn of light!

JOHN MILTON

# Auguries of Innocence

To see a World in a Grain of Sand
And a Heaven in a Wild Flower
Hold Infinity in the palm of your hand
And Eternity in an hour
A Robin Red breast in a Cage
Puts all Heaven in a Rage
A Dove house filld with Doves & Pigeons
Shudders Hell thr' all its regions
A dog starvd at his Masters Gate
Predicts the ruin of the State
A Horse misusd upon the Road
Calls to Heaven for Human blood
Each outcry of the hunted Hare
A fibre from the Brain does tear
A Skylark wounded in the wing
A Cherubim does cease to sing
The Game Cock clipd & armd for fight
Does the Rising Sun affright
Every Wolfs & Lions howl
Raises from Hell a Human Soul
The wild deer, wandring here & there
Keeps the Human Soul from Care
The Lamb misusd breeds Public Strife
And yet forgives the Butchers knife
The Bat that flits at close of Eve
Has left the Brain that wont Believe
The Owl that calls upon the Night
Speaks the Unbelievers fright

He who shall hurt the little Wren
Shall never be belovd by Men
He who the Ox to wrath has movd
Shall never be by Woman lovd
The wanton Boy that kills the Fly
Shall feel the Spiders enmity
He who torments the Chafers Sprite
Weaves a Bower in endless Night
The Catterpiller on the Leaf
Repeats to thee thy Mothers grief
Kill not the Moth nor Butterfly
For the Last Judgment draweth nigh
He who shall train the Horse to War
Shall never pass the Polar Bar
The Beggars Dog & Widows Cat
Feed them & thou wilt grow fat
The Gnat that sings his Summers Song
Poison gets from Slanders tongue
The poison of the Snake & Newt
Is the sweat of Envys Foot
The poison of the Honey Bee
Is the Artists Jealousy
The Princes Robes & Beggars Rags
Are Toadstools on the Misers Bags
A Truth thats told with bad intent
Beats all the Lies you can invent
It is right it should be so
Man was made for Joy & Woe
And when this we rightly know
Thro the World we safely go

Joy & Woe are woven fine
A Clothing for the soul divine
Under every grief & pine
Runs a joy with silken twine
The Babe is more than swadling Bands
Throughout all these Human Lands
Tools were made & Born were hands
Every Farmer Understands
Every Tear from Every Eye
Becomes a Babe in Eternity
This is caught by Females bright
And returnd to its own delight
The Bleat the Bark Bellow & Roar
Are Waves that Beat on Heavens Shore
The Babe that weeps the Rod beneath
Writes Revenge in realms of Death
The Beggars Rags fluttering in Air
Does to Rags the Heavens tear
The Soldier armd with Sword & Gun
Palsied strikes the Summers Sun
The poor Mans Farthing is worth more
Than all the Gold on Africs Shore
One Mite wrung from the Labrers hands
Shall buy & sell the Misers Lands
Or if protected from on high
Does that whole Nation sell & buy
He who mocks the Infants Faith
Shall be mockd in Age & Death
He who shall teach the Child to Doubt
The rotting Grave shall neer get out

He who respects the Infants faith
Triumphs over Hell & Death
The Childs Toys & the Old Mans Reasons
Are the Fruits of the Two seasons
The Questioner who sits so sly
Shall never know how to Reply
He who replies to words of Doubt
Doth put the Light of Knowledge out
The Strongest Poison ever known
Came from Caesars Laurel Crown
Nought can Deform the Human Race
Like to the Armours iron brace
When Gold & Gems adorn the Plow
To peaceful Arts shall Envy Bow
A Riddle or the Crickets Cry
Is to Doubt a fit Reply
The Emmets Inch & Eagles Mile
Make Lame Philosophy to smile
He who Doubts from what he sees
Will neer Believe do what you Please
If the Sun & Moon should Doubt
Theyd immediately Go out
To be in a Passion you Good may Do
But no Good if a Passion is in you
The Whore & Gambler by the State
Licencd build that Nations Fate
The Harlots cry from Street to Street
Shall weave Old Englands winding Sheet
The Winners Shout the Losers Curse
Dance before dead Englands Hearse

Every Night & every Morn
Some to Misery are Born
Every Morn and every Night
Some are Born to sweet delight
Some are Born to sweet delight
Some are Born to Endless Night
We are led to Believe a Lie
When we see not Thro the Eye
Which was Born in a Night to perish in a Night
When the Soul Slept in Beams of Light
God Appears & God is Light
To those poor Souls who dwell in Night
But does a Human Form Display
To those who Dwell in Realms of day

WILLIAM BLAKE

## The Matrix

Goaded and harassed in the factory
  That tears our life up into bits of days
  Ticked off upon a clock which never stays,
Shredding our portion of Eternity,
We break away at last, and steal the key
  Which hides a world empty of hours; ways
  Of space unroll, and Heaven overlays
The leafy, sun-lit earth of Fantasy.
  Beyond the ilex shadow glares the sun,
  Scorching against the blue flame of the sky.
Brown lily-pads lie heavy and supine
  Within a granite basin, under one
  The bronze-gold glimmer of a carp; and I
Reach out my hand and pluck a nectarine.

AMY LOWELL

## Soul and Body

Poor Soul, the centre of my sinful earth,
Fool'd by those rebel powers that thee array,
Why dost thou pine within, and suffer dearth,
Painting thy outward walls so costly gay?

Why so large cost, having so short a lease,
Dost thou upon thy fading mansion spend?
Shall worms, inheritors of this excess,
Eat up thy charge? is this thy body's end?

Then, Soul, live thou upon thy servant's loss,
And let that pine to aggravate thy store;
Buy terms divine in selling hours of dross;
Within be fed, without be rich no more:—

So shall thou feed on death, that feeds on men,
And death once dead, there's no more dying then.

WILLIAM SHAKESPEARE

# Wonder

How like an angel came I down!
How bright are all things here!
When first among his works I did appear
O how their glory me did crown!
The world resembled his eternity,
In which my soul did walk;
And ev'ry thing that I did see
Did with me talk.

The skies in their magnificence,
The lively, lovely air;
Oh how divine, how soft, how sweet, how fair!
The stars did entertain my sense,
And all the works of God, so bright and pure,
So rich and great did seem,
As if they ever must endure
In my esteem.

A native health and innocence
Within my bones did grow,
And while my God did all his glories show,
I felt a vigour in my sense
That was all spirit. I within did flow
With seas of life, like wine;
I nothing in the world did know
But 'twas divine.

Harsh ragged objects were conceal'd,
Oppressions tears and cries,
Sins, griefs, complaints, dissensions, weeping eyes
Were hid, and only things reveal'd
Which heav'nly spirits, and the angels prize.
The state of innocence
And bliss, not trades and poverties,
Did fill my sense.

The streets were pav'd with golden stones,
The boys and girls were mine,
Oh how did all their lovely faces shine!
The sons of men were holy ones,
In joy and beauty they appear'd to me,
And every thing which here I found,
While like an angel I did see,
Adorn'd the ground.

Rich diamond and pearl and gold
In ev'ry place was seen;
Rare splendours, yellow, blue, red, white and green,
Mine eyes did everywhere behold.
Great wonders cloth'd with glory did appear,
Amazement was my bliss,
That and my wealth was ev'ry where:
No joy to this!

Curs'd and devis'd proprieties,
With envy, avarice
And fraud, those fiends that spoil even Paradise,

Flew from the splendour of mine eyes,
And so did hedges, ditches, limits, bounds,
I dream'd not aught of those,
But wander'd over all men's grounds,
And found repose.

Proprieties themselves were mine,
And hedges ornaments;
Walls, boxes, coffers, and their rich contents
Did not divide my joys, but all combine.
Clothes, ribbons, jewels, laces, I esteem'd
My joys by others worn:
For me they all to wear them seem'd
When I was born.

THOMAS TRAHERNE

## A Dream of the Unknown

I dream'd that, as I wander'd by the way
 Bare Winter suddenly was changed to Spring,
And gentle odours led my steps astray,
 Mix'd with a sound of waters murmuring
Along a shelving bank of turf, which lay
 Under a copse, and hardly dared to fling
Its green arms round the bosom of the stream,
But kiss'd it and then fled, as Thou mightest in dream.

There grew pied wind-flowers and violets,
 Daisies, those pearl'd Arcturi of the earth,
The constellated flower that never sets;
 Faint oxlips; tender blue-bells, at whose birth
The sod scarce heaved; and that tall flower that wets
 Its mother's face with heaven-collected tears,
When the low wind, its playmate's voice, it hears.

And in the warm hedge grew lush eglantine,
 Green cow-bind and the moonlight-colour'd May,
And cherry-blossoms, and white cups, whose wine
 Was the bright dew yet drain'd not by the day;
And wild roses, and ivy serpentine,
 With its dark buds and leaves, wandering astray;
And flowers azure, black, and streak'd with gold,
Fairer than any waken'd eyes behold.

And nearer to the rivers trembling edge
 There grew broad flag-flowers, purple prankt with
     white,
And starry river-buds among the sedge,
 And floating water-lilies, broad and bright,
Which lit the oak that overhung the hedge
 With moonlight beams of their own watery light;
And bulrushes, and reeds of such deep green
As soothed the dazzled eye with sober sheen.

Methought that of these visionary flowers
 I made a nosegay, bound in such a way
That the same hues, which in their natural bowers
 Were mingled or opposed, the like array
Kept these imprison'd children of the Hours
 Within my hand;—and then, elate and gay,
I hasten'd to the spot whence I had come
That I might there present it—O! to Whom?

PERCY BYSSHE SHELLEY

## If Spirits Walk

*"I have heard (but not believed) the spirits of the dead*
*May walk again."*
*Winter's Tale*

If spirits walk, Love, when the night climbs slow
The slant footpath where we were wont to go,
    Be sure that I shall take the self-same way
    To the hill-crest, and shoreward, down the gray,
Sheer, gravelled slope, where vetches straggling grow.

Look for me not when gusts of winter blow,
When at thy pane beat hands of sleet and snow;
   I would not come thy dear eyes to affray,
       If spirits walk.

But when, in June, the pines are whispering low,
And when their breath plays with thy bright hair so
    As some one's fingers once were used to play—
    That hour when birds leave song, and children pray,
Keep the old tryst, sweetheart, and thou shalt know
       If spirits walk.

SOPHIE JEWETT

## Whatever Is

Whatever is we only know
As in our minds we find it so;
No staring fact is half so clear
As one dim, preconceived idea --
No matter how the fact may glow.

Vainly may Truth her trumpet blow
To stir our minds; like heavy dough
They stick to what they think — won't hear
Whatever is.

Our ancient myths in solid row
Stand up — we simply have to go
And choke each fiction old and dear
Before the modest facts appear;
Then we may grasp, reluctant, slow,
Whatever is.

CHARLOTTE ANNA PERKINS GILMAN

# Vision

I have not walked on common ground,
Nor drunk of earthly streams;
A shining figure, mailed and crowned,
Moves softly through my dreams.

He makes the air so keen and strange,
The stars so fiercely bright;
The rocks of time, the tides of change,
Are nothing in his sight.

Death lays no shadow on his smile;
Life is a race fore-run;
Look in his face a little while,
And life and death are one.

MARJORIE PICKTHALL

## There May Be Chaos Still Around the World

There may be chaos still around the world,
This little world that in my thinking lies;
For mine own bosom is the paradise
Where all my life's fair visions are unfurled.
Within my nature's shell I slumber curled,
Unmindful of the changing outer skies,
Where now, perchance, some new-born Eros flies,
Or some old Cronos from his throne is hurled.
I heed them not; or if the subtle night
Haunt me with deities I never saw,
I soon mine eyelid's drowsy curtain draw
To hide their myriad faces from my sight.
They threat in vain; the whirlwind cannot awe
A happy snow-flake dancing in the flaw.

GEORGE SANTAYANA

## I Am the Only Being Whose Doom

I am the only being whose doom
No tongue would ask, no eye would mourn;
I never caused a thought of gloom,
A smile of joy, since I was born.

In secret pleasure, secret tears,
This changeful life has slipped away,
As friendless after eighteen years,
As lone as on my natal day.

There have been times I cannot hide,
There have been times when this was drear,
When my sad soul forgot its pride
And longed for one to love me here.

But those were in the early glow
Of feelings since subdued by care;
And they have died so long ago,
I hardly now believe they were.

First melted off the hope of youth,
Then fancy's rainbow fast withdrew;
And then experience told me truth
In mortal bosoms never grew.

'Twas grief enough to think mankind
All hollow, servile, insincere;
But worse to trust to my own mind
And find the same corruption there.

EMILY BRONTË

# Solitude

Laugh, and the world laughs with you;
Weep, and you weep alone;
For the sad old earth must borrow its mirth,
But has trouble enough of its own.
Sing, and the hills will answer;
Sigh, it is lost on the air;
The echoes bound to a joyful sound,
But shrink from voicing care.

Rejoice, and men will seek you;
Grieve, and they turn and go;
They want full measure of all your pleasure,
But they do not need your woe.
Be glad, and your friends are many;
Be sad, and you lose them all,—
There are none to decline your nectared wine,
But alone you must drink life's gall.

Feast, and your halls are crowded;
Fast, and the world goes by.
Succeed and give, and it helps you live,
But no man can help you die.
There is room in the halls of pleasure
For a large and lordly train,
But one by one we must all file on
Through the narrow aisles of pain.

ELLA WHEELER WILCOX

# And, the Last Day Being Come, Man Stood Alone

And, the last day being come, Man stood alone
Ere sunrise on the world's dismantled verge,
Awaiting how from everywhere should urge
The Coming of the Lord. And, behold, none

Did come,—but indistinct from every realm
Of earth and air and water, growing more
And louder, shriller, heavier, a roar
Up the dun atmosphere did overwhelm

His ears; and as he looked affrighted round
Every manner of beast innumerable
All thro' the shadows crying grew, until
The wailing was like grass upon the ground.

Asudden then within his human side
Their anguish, since the goad he wielded first,
And, since he gave them not to drink, their thirst,
Darted compressed and vital.—As he died,

Low in the East now lighting gorgeously
He saw the last sea-serpent iris-mailed
Which, with a spear transfixèd, yet availed
To pluck the sun down into the dead sea.

TRUMBULL STICKNEY

# Contents

## Travel and Discovery

## Mother Nature

**Passion**

**Spirituality**

Designed in Sydney, Australia

Printed in Canton, PRC

© 2021 The Shepherd Moon